small group bibl

G000123053

Living
empowered for ministry

The gifts of the Spirit

Florence MacKenzie

Scripture Union, 207–209 Queensway, Bletchley, MK2 2EB, England.
email: info@scriptureunion.org.uk
web site: www.scriptureunion.org.uk

We are an international Christian charity working with churches in more than 130 countries providing resources to bring the good news about Jesus Christ to children, young people and families – and to encourage them to develop spiritually through the Bible and prayer.

As well as our network of volunteers, staff and associates who run holidays, church-based events and school Christian groups, we produce a wide range of publications and support those who use our resources through training programmes.

British Library Cataloguing-in-Publication Data

A catalogue record for this book is available from the British Library.

Cover design: Carsten Lorenz

Printed in Great Britain by Ebenezer Baylis & Son Ltd, The Trinity Press, Worcester and London.

Contents

To Laura and Dave: these gifts are much better than birthday presents! Open all the ones with your name on and then take every opportunity to use them – he's worth it!

| Introduction

Every part of the Bible is God's word to human beings – even parts which might be difficult to understand or which cause controversy. The passages on spiritual gifts are no exception and, despite the differences of opinion which exist among Christians, I think we have a lot to learn from what the Bible says about this matter. Christian opinion is, sadly, often one of extremes - on the one hand, there is a sincerely held view that the gifts of the Spirit were intended only for the church in New Testament times and that all, or at least some of these gifts, have now ceased to exist. On the other hand, a view which is just as sincerely held is that some gifts eg gifts of healing, miracles and tongues, are more desirable than others and these are often elevated at the expense of the other gifts. Is there a middle ground in between these two perspectives? I believe there is, and it is from this vantage point that this study is written. I suggest several reasons for this view:

◆ Nowhere in the Bible do we specifically read that any of the spiritual gifts have ceased.

◆ Nowhere in the Bible do we read that gifts of healing, miracles and tongues are more important or desirable than other gifts. In fact, in 1 Corinthians 14, the apostle Paul takes great pains to communicate to the Corinthian church the limitations and lesser importance of the gift of tongues compared to some of the other gifts.

◆ Nowhere in the Bible are we encouraged to seek the gift of tongues.

◆ Today's Christian believers – the church – are in as much need of being spiritually gifted (as opposed to being naturally talented) as the church in New Testament times.

◆ One of God's purposes is to strengthen his church – Jesus' promise to build his church (Matthew 16:18) is still being worked out today, and one way in which this is happening is through spiritually gifted Christians.

◆ The mission of the church today – to make disciples and to teach them

(Matthew 28:19) – is no different from the church in New Testament times; part of fulfilling this mission is to use the materials the Lord has provided for us – spiritual gifts.

A recurring theme throughout this study is the importance of discussing and exercising spiritual gifts in love. For each spiritual gift discussed in this study, there is a section called 'for private reflection'. In each case, there is a reminder to consider the content of 1 Corinthians 13. Love is supremely important in the area of spiritual gifts because, without it, jealousy, bickering, and division will soon take over. None of the spiritual gifts were meant to divide – their purpose is to build up the body of Christ, the church.

As you begin this study, I encourage you to be open to what the Lord is teaching you through his Spirit. It might mean you'll have to give up views which you've held for a long time; if so, it's only because he wants to lead you into all truth (John 16:13). Trust him to guide your thinking and your responses throughout this study – believe me, he knows what he's doing!

How to use this study

Welcome to this study of the gifts of the Spirit! My desire is that as you study and share your findings with others, you will be drawn into a closer relationship with the Lord.

This Bible study has two main aims: the first is to encourage you to dig deep into the Word of God because this is our main guide for living, and the second is to help you apply this Word to your daily life. Only God's Word is completely trustworthy and, if we are going to live in a way that will honour and please him, then we need to know what he says in the Bible. However, being merely familiar with what the Bible says is, in itself, insufficient. In order for God's Word to be real and vital in our lives, there needs to be application of the truths that we read about there. The best way to do this is to cooperate with the Holy Spirit. Ask him to help you take on board what God is saying to you in the Bible. Ask him to apply his Word to you so that there is no way that you can remain unchanged by its power. Biblical truth applied to our lives by the Holy Spirit results in spiritual growth and changed attitudes and behaviour.

This study is for either individual or group application. If you are sharing your answers with others in a group, this is a wonderful way to support and encourage one another. However, the most important part of the study is in preparation. Allow yourself plenty of time to read the questions and the Bible references. Get alone with the Lord and his Word. Ask him for his help as you go through each of the questions. Don't concern yourself about 'wrong answers' – do as much as you can, as completely as you can. This is really your learning period. Fully prepared in this way, you will find that you will receive immense benefit from the subsequent sharing in your group. You will also be in a much stronger position to contribute thoughtfully and meaningfully – this will be greatly appreciated by both your leader and other group members.

The time taken in preparation will vary from person to person. Don't be concerned if it takes a while to complete each chapter. My intention is that the questions and Bible verses will cause you to linger in the Lord's presence. However, I suggest you avoid the temptation of answering all the questions from a chapter in one sitting the day or evening before you meet with the rest of your group to share what you have written. It might overwhelm you to tackle a whole chapter at a time. Instead, you'll probably find it helpful to divide up each chapter into study sections. For example, each one is already divided into three parts. Depending on the frequency with which your group meets, you might wish to do each section over two days, giving a six day preparation time, with about twenty minutes per day devoted to answering the questions, reading the Bible verses and praying about the application to your own life. This could be a suitable pattern if your group meets every week. On the other hand, if you meet with others every two weeks, you could complete the study by spending around twenty minutes every other day, or by spending less time each day but preparing your answers over a ten or twelve day period. The way you prepare is essentially up to you – different people have varying needs and responsibilities – but the important thing is that you develop a pattern of study which works for you and then stick to it! If you haven't approached Bible study in this way before, I'm sure you'll find that the discipline it involves will be extremely helpful in your everyday life.

I trust that you will discover the gift(s) which the Lord has given you – and then joyfully develop it in his service and in the building up of others in the church.

Notes for leaders

Leading a Bible study is a great privilege and responsibility. Not only do leaders need to thoroughly prepare the study material, but they also need to prepare themselves. This involves being in a close relationship with the Lord, arising out of personal Bible study and prayer, along with a commitment to live their lives to God's glory. No matter how much natural talent leaders might have, they are absolutely dependent upon the Lord for wisdom and help in leading their groups. My desire is that, as you study this material together with your group members, you will draw your strength from him and will become more like him.

Encourage your group members to write down their answers to the questions before coming to the Bible study meeting. In my own experience as group leader, and in talking with other leaders, I've found this to be a vital part of Christian growth. Preparation allows an opportunity to be guided by the Holy Spirit in answering the questions, whereas an 'off-the-cuff' response during the meeting, with no prayerful preparation time, is less likely to be helpful to others in the group. Asking that all members of your group prepare each chapter in advance of your meeting helps to encourage timid, less knowledgeable members to contribute their responses on a more equal footing with spiritually mature members – this, in turn, can lead to greater spiritual growth and unity within the group.

This Bible study will take about sixty to ninety minutes to discuss people's answers to the questions. It's important that all questions are covered in your meeting, because if you get into the habit of not discussing the final questions in each chapter, your members might not prepare answers to these questions for future chapters. I suggest, therefore, that you prepare a time schedule in advance of your meeting – write down your start time at the beginning, then the time you expect to complete the first section, and the second section, and finally the third section of the chapter to be discussed. In this way, you should be able to keep track of your time and know whether you need to slow down or speed up in discussing your group's responses.

May the Lord be constantly at your side as you seek to lead others into a deeper knowledge of him.

1| Who is the Holy Spirit?

'We have not received the spirit of the world but the Spirit who is from God, that we may understand what God has freely given us.'
1 Corinthians 2:12

In order to be true to the teachings of Scripture, I need to understand who the Holy Spirit is. Since He is God, I need to give Him the recognition, worship, and praise that God deserves. If I do not know who the Holy Spirit is, I will not enjoy a proper relationship with Him or have His full ministry in my life.
Max Anders [1]

'You're going to write a Bible study on *what*? Well, that won't be easy – you know that there are genuine Christian believers whose views on this are miles apart! How on earth are you going to manage it?' This sort of comment did nothing for my confidence when I decided to write a study on the gifts of the Spirit. Perhaps I should choose an easier topic, I thought – one that was less controversial. But we should never shy away from anything which we're taught in the Bible – the problem here, I think, is not so much with what the Bible teaches, but rather with people's *interpretations* of what the Bible teaches! Before looking at the subject of spiritual gifts, I'd like us to begin our study by focusing on the giver of the gifts – the Holy Spirit.

Who is *he*?

Perhaps the most common mistake regarding the Spirit is perceiving Him as power and not a person, a force with no identity. Such is not

true. The Holy Spirit is a person… He has knowledge (1 Cor 2:11). He has a will (1 Cor 12:11). He has a mind (Romans 8:27). He has affections (Romans 15:30). You can lie to Him (Acts 5:3–4). You can insult Him (Hebrews 10:29). You can grieve Him (Ephes 4:30).
Max Lucado [2]

As we become familiar with God's Word, the Bible, we learn that the one true God is Father, Son (Jesus Christ), and Holy Spirit. It's important to stress that we believe in one God and not three separate gods. It's difficult to find an illustration which explains this adequately. In the introduction to one of my other studies, *Living out the life of Jesus*, I use the example of a triangle, which has three sides yet is one shape. If we think of the example of the first disciples, they began by worshipping God above them (the Father). They then got to know God alongside them (the Son, Jesus). Finally they experienced God within them (the Holy Spirit).

Read Matthew 28:19; Luke 1:35; 2 Corinthians 13:14

Q Write down what each tells you about the three-in-one God.

What does *he* do?

While the role that the Holy Spirit desires to have in our lives is enormous, many believers do not begin to allow Him to work. Whether through fear, ignorance, or sin, they have effectively hindered Him. Most of us have only begun to explore the works God yearns to do in our lives by His Holy Spirit! Don't be afraid to give Him freedom to work. Your life will never be the same!
Craig Keener [3]

We learn from the Bible that the Holy Spirit is involved in many different activities. Look up the references given below and match them up with the correct description of the Spirit's work.

	Verses	Descriptions of the Spirit's work	
3	John 16:7	Gives understanding	1
7	John 16:8	Lives inside us	2
4	John 16:13	Counsels and helps us	3
8	Romans 8:16	Leads us into all truth	4
6	Romans 8:26	Produces fruit	5
1	1 Cor 2:12	Prays for us	6
2	1 Cor 3:16	Convicts of sin, righteousness and judgement	7
9	1 Cor 12:11	Assures us we are God's children	8
5	Gal 5:22,23	Gives gifts	9

Q Do you find any of these surprising? Share with your group the reasons for your answer.

Q Choose at least one of these aspects of the Spirit's work and, again, share with the rest of your group the encouragement which this brings you.

Q Look again at the descriptions of the Spirit's work in the above table. In all the above Jesus said that 'He will bring glory to me by taking from what is mine and making it known to you.' Read John 16:14–15. What does this tell you about the Spirit's relation to the Father and the Son?

Q How real is the Holy Spirit to you? How often do you acknowledge all the work he does on your behalf? *Take time now* to thank him that he is God; give him praise for what he's doing in your life right now; and give him permission to do more in your life in the future by surrendering your plans to his control and direction.

The Gift of the Holy Spirit

Satan has opposed the doctrine of the Spirit-filled life about as bitter-ly as any other doctrine there is. He has confused it, opposed it, sur-rounded it with false notions and fears ... The Spirit-filled life is not a special, deluxe edition of Christianity. It is part and parcel of the total plan of God for His people ... There is nothing about the Holy Spirit queer or strange or eerie.
A W Tozer 4

All Christian believers have been at the point where they realise that they just can't make it on their own. No matter how hard they try to live a good life, it's not going to be good enough to satisfy God. He demands perfection, but we can't give it to him. All is not lost, however, because God's Son – Jesus Christ – lived and died to bring us into a right relation-ship with him. Our responsibility is to believe that his perfect sacrifice was acceptable to God and to turn from our sins to begin a life of obedience to what he teaches in the Bible. This is what the Bible describes as being 'born again' (John 3:3). After we've been born again, ie become Christian believers, God doesn't leave us to our own devices. At the moment we become Christians, he gives us his Holy Spirit.

Read Acts 2:38; 1 Corinthians 3:16

Q Write down what they say about this.

After we become Christians, we grow more like Jesus by increasingly giving up control of our lives to God's Spirit. We have a choice – to live according to our own desires and plans without reference to the Spirit within us, or to allow the Spirit to set the agenda for our lives by giving him the freedom to direct and empower us from day to day.

Read Ephesians 5:18

Q Write down the phrase that describes those who are yielded to the Holy Spirit's control in their lives.

We know from the Bible that the Holy Spirit lives within every Christian believer, yet not every Christian is filled with the Spirit. Sadly, we're very reluctant to allow him to fill or take control of every area of our lives because we're often content to have Jesus just as our Saviour – we think it might be too costly for us to submit to him as Lord on a consistent daily basis. However, we are commanded to 'be filled with the Spirit'. The original sense of this verse means to *keep on being filled* with the Spirit – it is a process by which we continually allow the Spirit to guide and empower us. What do we learn from the fact that this is a command?

The instruction to be filled with the Spirit tells us that the Lord wants this for *all* Christians (not just those in prominent ministry positions); that it's possible to obey; and that we're accountable to him if we ignore this clear command. There are several reasons why many Christians are not filled with the Spirit and are therefore living at less than God's best for them. Let's have a look at two of these reasons.

We're not prepared to face up to sins in our lives.

Every Christian has an 'old' nature which wants to indulge in sin, as well as a 'new' nature which wants to live in a way that pleases God. There is a constant battle going on between these two natures.

Read Romans 8:5–8

Q What do you learn from these verses?

In a battle, the stronger side usually wins. One way in which physical strength is built up is by eating the right kind of food. Similarly, we can strengthen our new nature by 'feeding' it with the right sort of things. The more we 'feed' our new nature, the more we 'starve' our old nature. Look at the following list of suggestions. Put an 'N' beside those which are likely to strengthen our new nature and an 'O' beside those which are likely to strengthen our old nature.

N ◆ Admit and turn away from all known sin in our lives – the Bible calls this confession and repentance.

O ◆ Be careless about what we read or watch on TV, video, etc.

O ◆ Neglect a daily time alone with God.

iV ◆ Spend time worshipping with other Christians.

O ◆ Deliberately place ourselves in situations where we're likely to be tempted to sin.

iV ◆ Apply Philippians 4:8 on a regular basis.

O ◆ Have a grumbling, complaining attitude.

iV ◆ Take opportunities to share with others what God has done in our lives.

Are there sins in your life which you've not had the courage to face up to? They may be small or large but, either way, they're blocking the effectiveness of the Holy Spirit's work in and through you. God's Spirit can't fill you if your life is clogged with sinful desires and behaviour patterns. Facing up to your sins will mean admitting that you're not as good as you thought you were. It will also mean you have to stop tolerating these sins in your life and begin to turn your back on them by repenting of them. *Take time now* to set the record straight between yourself and the Lord – he's so willing to forgive you and to make you useful for him again.

We're not prepared to submit to God by putting ourselves at his disposal for him to use as he wishes.

Read Romans 6:13; Romans 12:1; James 4:7

Q Write down what they tell us about submitting or yielding to God.

Q Choose one of the above verses and be specific as to how you can apply it in a practical way.

Confession and repentance might be described as the negative side of submission; this involves getting rid of everything which hinders God's control over our lives. Yielding to God might be described as the positive side; this involves placing ourselves totally and com-

pletely (as best we know how) into the hands of God in complete submission to His will for our lives.
Billy Graham [5]

When Christians allow the Holy Spirit to take control of every part of their lives, they become fruitful. Spirit-filled Christians will bear the fruit of the Spirit on a consistent basis.

Read Galatians 5:22,23

Q Write down the nine characteristics which, taken together, make up this fruit.

It's not your responsibility to produce the fruit – that's the work of the Spirit – but you need to bear or demonstrate this fruit in your life. The fruit comes from a close relationship with the Lord – read John 15:1–8 to remind yourself of this, and make sure you stay connected to him.

Why do you think we've taken so much time to consider the importance of Christians being filled with the Spirit *before* we go on to study the gifts of the Spirit?

The filling of the Holy Spirit should not be a once-for-all event, but a continuous reality every day of our lives. It is a process. We must surrender ourselves to Him daily, and every day we must choose to remain surrendered … We are already the temple of God, indwelt by the Holy Spirit, but He wants to fill us. However, He can fill only those who wish to be emptied of self and yielded to Him. Therefore, this active surrender must continue day by day, concerning little things as well as big ones.
Billy Graham [6]

Personal comment

Have you ever gone to a building site hoping to see some new house designs, only to be disappointed because the builders hadn't progressed beyond the

foundations stage? Although we recognise the importance of solid founda-
tions for buildings, we're not very keen to spend a lot of time looking at them
– we'd much rather come on the scene when the house is more advanced
and we can then admire the different designs. I think that a study on the gifts
of the Spirit is a bit like that – we want to dive straight in and look at all the
different 'designs' of gifts and give little or no consideration to the foundation
on which a biblical study of the gifts must be based. Jesus knew the impor-
tance of good foundations – he's pretty clear about this in Matthew 7:24–27.
In the same way, we've laid a foundation for this study. Our foundation is
what the Bible tells us about the divine person of the Holy Spirit and his work.
In order to have an understanding of the Spirit's gifts which doesn't crumble
as soon as we look at them, we need this firm foundation. Although I'm
looking forward to studying the various gifts of the Spirit, I think it's impor-
tant to get them in perspective. First of all, we need to remind ourselves that
all Christian believers have the Holy Spirit living in them, but not all
Christians give up the control of their lives to him on a daily basis – in other
words, they are not filled with the Spirit. It's only as we continue to obey
biblical commands and submit to God's will and purposes for our lives that
we are filled and go on being filled. But where do the gifts fit in? Well, think of
it this way. Imagine twin boys are celebrating their birthday and have just
been given presents by their father. One child is unruly and impatient, and
takes the gift without even saying 'thank you'. He imagines the gift is for his
satisfaction alone and he doesn't want to share it with any of his friends.
However, the boy soon gets bored and starts wanting another gift.

The second child thanks his father for the gift, even though he hasn't yet
unwrapped it. He knows it will be a good gift and he has no need to be fright-
ened of it because he trusts his father's kindness. He opens his gift and imme-
diately asks his father how he should use it. The child stays close to where his
father is so that he can hear what his father is saying. The boy is grateful for
the gift and is keen to share it with his friends. He doesn't focus all his atten-
tion on the gift, however; he is more concerned with having a good relation-
ship with his father and pleasing him. It is against the backdrop of this close
relationship that he will be able to put his gift to good use.

Does this help you to understand the place of spiritual gifts in the life of
Christians? We must always focus on the Giver; we must use our spiritual
gift(s) in the context of a close, obedient relationship of willing submission to
the Holy Spirit; and we must be ready to accept whatever gift he wants to give
us.

2| Spiritual gifts – What do I need to know?

'Now about spiritual gifts, brothers, I do not want you to be ignorant.'
1 Corinthians 12:1

The truth of the matter is that the Scriptures plainly imply the imperative of possessing the gifts of the Spirit ... (1 Corinthians 12:31; 1 Corinthians 14:1). It does not appear to be an optional matter with us but rather a scriptural mandate to those who have been filled with the Spirit.
A W Tozer [1]

The box in which it was packed didn't give us any clues. In fact, it was obvious the gift had been packed in the wrong box! None of our other wedding presents had caused us any difficulty, but this one – well, we just couldn't work out what it was! It was made of glass and looked like some sort of plate with an arched metal handle, but what it was supposed to be used for was anyone's guess! In order for gifts to serve their proper function, we have to be clear what they are and how they're to be used. The same is true of spiritual gifts. We have to know what they are and how God intends us to use them. However, before we dive straight in and tear off the wrapping paper, let's start this chapter by looking at how gifts relate to talents; to the church; and to you.

Gifts and talents

Spiritual gifts are special abilities distributed by the Holy Spirit to every believer according to God's design and grace for the common good of the body of Christ.
Bruce Bugbee *et al* [2]

'He's a gifted speaker.'

'She's a gifted musician.'

'I wish I had her talent for cooking!'

'He's such a talented sportsman.'

No doubt you've heard similar statements about people with particular abilities. 'Gifts' and 'talents' are sometimes used interchangeably, but how correct is this when we're talking about *spiritual* gifts? Are spiritual gifts nothing more than Christian talents? Can someone develop a spiritual gift in an area where they showed no talent before they became a Christian? If a person is naturally talented in a particular area, does this mean this talent becomes a spiritual gift when they trust in the Lord? Read the following list and place (G) beside those statements you think are spiritual gifts, and (T) beside those you think are natural talents.

◆ An unbelieving person plays the piano to a high degree of proficiency

◆ A Christian receives excellent ratings from her students at the university where she teaches modern languages

◆ A Christian communicates biblical truth in such a way that spiritual growth consistently results in those who hear him.

◆ An individual has inherited from his father and grandfather the ability to sing well

◆ A supernatural enabling of the Holy Spirit which equips a Christian to serve and minister to others.

Spiritual gifts are not the same as talents. Both believers and unbelievers can be talented, but only Christians can have spiritual gifts. Talents can be present from a very young age, spiritual gifts only when a person becomes a Christian. Some talents may be inherited, spiritual gifts are given directly by the Holy Spirit. Talents benefit people on a natural level, spiritual gifts on a spiritual level – people in the church are built up spiritually through a Christian exercising the gift of encouragement. A Christian might be talented in a particular area, such as teaching, but the same person might not have the spiritual gift of teaching. Conversely, someone with no natural talent for teaching might have the spiritual gift of teaching. In other cases, the Spirit gives a gift where there is already natural talent in that particular area.

Gifts and the church

When the apostle Paul talks about spiritual gifts, it's always in the context of his letters to Christian believers in various churches, ie at Rome, Corinth, and Ephesus. Look at the table below which lists the gifts mentioned in each of these letters.

Rom 12:6–8	1 Cor 12:8–10, 28	Eph 4:11
Prophecy	Prophecy	Prophecy
Service		
Teaching	Teaching	Teaching
Encouragement		
Giving		
Leadership		
Mercy		
	(Word of) wisdom	
	(Word of) knowledge	
	Faith	
	Healing	
	Miracles	
	Discernment	
	Tongues	
	Interpret tongues	
	Apostleship	Apostleship
	Helps	
	Administration	
		Evangelism
		Pastoring

Notice that the list to each church is different – none of them received exactly the same information on spiritual gifts. Only the gifts of teaching and prophecy are mentioned to all three churches; the gift of apostleship is mentioned to two of them; while the majority of gifts are recorded only once.

It should be understood that whilst they are helpful guides, these lists are not exhaustive.

The lists can serve as a helpful guideline, giving us ideas about the kinds of gifts God gives. They can also affirm that gifts we have identified in ourselves are important to the Body of Christ. But if other believers are consistently built up by an ability you have that is not on one of the lists, relax. Who is to say that God doesn't also give the gift of youth work, or worship leading, or counselling? The key is to find the areas in which the Holy Spirit seems to supernaturally empower your service to others, and to focus your efforts there.
Susan Maycinik [3]

Nowhere in the Bible do we read of spiritual gifts being given for personal satisfaction or personal advancement.

Read 1 Corinthians 12:7; Ephesians 4:12,13

Q Write down the purpose of the gifts.

In his letters to the Roman, Corinthian and Ephesian Christians, Paul uses the analogy of the human body.

Read Romans 12:4–6a; 1 Corinthians 12:12–27; Ephesians 4:11–13

Q Write down how these repeated references to the body help you to understand how spiritual gifts work together in the life of the church.

Q Remaining with the body analogy, what do you think happens to a church when some members don't exercise their spiritual gifts?

Q Read 1 Corinthians 12:12–27 again. This passage brings out the importance of both unity and diversity within the Christian church. How might the use of diverse gifts produce unity in a church? Use real or imaginary church situations to illustrate your answer.

We are all diverse, but we are called to serve without division ...
Unity is not achieved by being alike ... God has designed each part
of the body to be in an interdependent relationship with all the other
parts.
Bruce Bugbee *et al* 4

As we exercise our spiritual gifts 'as a means of helping the entire church' (1 Corinthians 12:7, NLT), we should do this with lives which are fully surrendered to the Holy Spirit. In our eagerness to find out about and to apply our spiritual gifts, we shouldn't overlook the importance of the Lord's command in John 15:4,5 to remain closely connected to him. Spiritual gifts should never become more important than spiritual fruit. One of the fruit segments in Galatians 5:22 is love. It's no coincidence, therefore, that in the middle of Paul's discussion about spiritual gifts to the Corinthian church (1 Corinthians 12 and 14), there is that wonderful 'love chapter', chapter 13. This chapter shows us 'the most excellent way' to use our spiritual gifts – the way of love.

Read 1 Corinthians 13

Q Identify the spiritual gifts mentioned there.

Q How could some of the principles mentioned in verses 4–7 be applied in the exercise of spiritual gifts?

As you begin this study on the gifts of the Spirit, ask the Lord to remind you of the importance of love in discussing and exercising gifts. When you find that your interpretation of some of the gifts is different from that of another Christian in your Bible study group, remember and apply the love principles of 1 Corinthians 13. This will thoroughly annoy Satan, but will delight the Lord.

This so-called hymn to love was Paul's prescription for solving the sickness in the church body in Corinth. The believers had spiritual gifts, but they lacked spiritual graces and needed to be reminded why love is so important in the Christian life.
Warren W Wiersbe [5]

Gifts and you

Be open to the Holy Spirit surprising you with gifts outside of your normal operating range: You may have a certain gift mix at one point in your life – down the road it may be different according to how the Holy Spirit directs.
Jim Burns and Doug Fields [6]

Being part of the body of Christ means, first of all, that you are a Christian believer who has a living relationship with Jesus Christ. It also involves belonging to a group of Christians who worship and serve God together, with Jesus as the head. We've already seen how the church is like a body with many parts, each with its own specific function, but working *inter-dependently* with all the other parts. The question you're probably asking now is, 'How do I get to know what *my* part is in this body?' The following flow diagram might help to get you started.

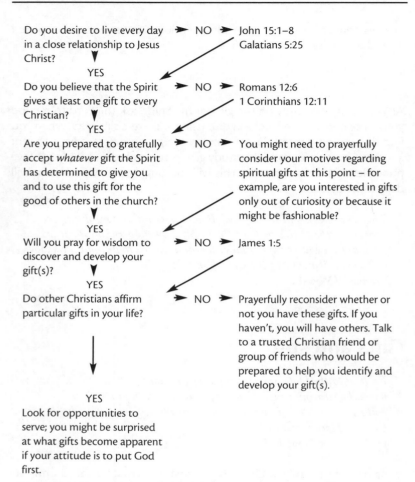

Do you desire to live every day in a close relationship to Jesus Christ? → NO → John 15:1–8 / Galatians 5:25

YES

Do you believe that the Spirit gives at least one gift to every Christian? → NO → Romans 12:6 / 1 Corinthians 12:11

YES

Are you prepared to gratefully accept *whatever* gift the Spirit has determined to give you and to use this gift for the good of others in the church? → NO → You might need to prayerfully consider your motives regarding spiritual gifts at this point – for example, are you interested in gifts only out of curiosity or because it might be fashionable?

YES

Will you pray for wisdom to discover and develop your gift(s)? → NO → James 1:5

YES

Do other Christians affirm particular gifts in your life? → NO → Prayerfully reconsider whether or not you have these gifts. If you haven't, you will have others. Talk to a trusted Christian friend or group of friends who would be prepared to help you identify and develop your gift(s).

YES

Look for opportunities to serve; you might be surprised at what gifts become apparent if your attitude is to put God first.

Sometimes we need to heed the Nike advert *'Just Do It!'* before we can be certain about what gift(s) the Spirit has given to us. Hands-on experience will often determine whether or not we're gifted in a particular area. At all times, we need to be tuned in to how the Lord wants us to serve him with other members of his body, remembering that our *attitude* towards our service is of paramount importance.

Read Psalm 40:8. Can you honestly say that, in the area of spiritual gifts, you desire to do God's will? Is the most important thing for you to please the Lord and to serve other Christians? Or are you interested in spiritual gifts solely for your own benefit, to increase your own importance or self-esteem? *Take time now* to pray about your answers to these questions.

There is always the danger that the person who believes God has given him or her a good sprinkling of spiritual gifts will fall captive to that old enemy, self-importance. God does not value us primarily for what we can do – even what we can do in His strength. He values us primarily for what He makes us, character-wise, conforming us to Christ by His grace.
J I Packer 7

Personal comment

How well do you know the Old Testament book of Proverbs? I think it's a wonderful book which gives a very shrewd perspective on contemporary life. In chapter 30, verse 8, we read, '... give me neither poverty nor riches ...' Here, the author is praying to be protected from the extremes of being very poor or of being very rich. We need to watch we don't fall victim to extremism when it comes to spiritual gifts. What do I mean? Well, there's the view that says we should always operate within the context of our gifts because God made us in such a way that there's a role in the body of Christ that only we can fill. On the other hand, there's the argument which suggests that focusing on spiritual gifts draws our attention away from the needs of others and on to ourselves and our own capabilities. Hmm... I don't think either of these two positions seems to be particularly biblical, do you? The Bible encourages us to use our spiritual gifts – 1 Corinthians is very clear about this, and the parable in Matthew 25:14–30 is pretty direct when it comes to the importance of responsibly using what God has given us. So, what's the solution? Like so many things, the answer lies in keeping a balanced perspective. Yes, we should find out what our spiritual gifts are and use them to build up the body of Christ. However, we shouldn't get so bogged down in defining what are/are not our gifts that we ignore a pressing need in the church if there's no one else who is gifted to meet that need. I think we should remind ourselves of Romans 12:1 'offer your bodies as living sacrifices, holy and pleasing to God'. Here's a picture of total commitment, where the focus is on pleasing God. Often, we'll do this by using the gifts he has given us; at other times, it will involve sacrifice – and that might mean, on occasion, serving outside our comfort zone and our areas of giftedness. What do you think?

3| Directing God's people

'Now there are varieties of gifts, but the same Spirit. And there are varieties of ministries, and the same Lord. And there are varieties of effects, but the same God who works all things in all persons.'
1 Corinthians 12:4–6 (NASB)

A true exercise of spiritual gifts in the church is not marked by flamboyant or spectacular manifestations, but by dedicated service. We can experience New Testament community only through the responsible use of the gifts of the Holy Spirit in mutual edification.
Kenneth C Kinghorn [1]

How good are you at organising the various things you have to do every day? I find it helps if I can group things together. I can listen to my friend's audio tape while I'm travelling in the car to collect my daughter from school and I can pick up the dry cleaning en route – three tasks done in one! But sometimes it's not easy to see the best way to arrange our activities. This is certainly true in discussing spiritual gifts. Which ones do you study first? Should they be taken in the order in which they appear in the Bible? Is it a good idea to arrange them alphabetically? Can they be grouped in some meaningful way? Well, I don't think there's any entirely satisfactory way of grouping the gifts into categories but, in order to make this study manageable, this is what we're going to do. I've settled for the twenty spiritual gifts mentioned in Romans, 1 Corinthians, and Ephesians. There may be more, there may be less, but for our purposes we'll stick with these twenty. I've decided to look at the gifts under seven headings, with a chapter dedicated to each heading. In this chapter, we're going to look at the gifts which are needed in directing God's people – administration, leadership and apostleship.

Gift of administration

This administrative task (Acts 6:1–7) was not taken lightly. Notice the requirements for the men who were to handle the food pro-gramme: they were to be well respected and full of the Holy Spirit and wisdom. People who carry heavy responsibilities and work close-ly with others should have these qualities. We must look for spiritu-ally mature and wise men and women to lead our churches.
Life Application Study Bible 2

'And in the church God has appointed ... those with gifts of administra-tion ...' (1 Corinthians 12:28).

A good definition of the gift of administration is the God-given *'ability to organise information, events, or material to work efficiently for the Body of Christ'.3* Spiritual gifts are normally defined within a New Testament context and are given in order to build up the body of Christ, ie Christian believers. We mustn't forget, though, that the Old Testament is also part of God's revealed Word and, as such, we shouldn't be surprised to see examples there of godly people who were obviously spiritually gifted in order to carry out a task God had given them to do.

Q One example of an Old Testament character who had the gift of administration is Joseph (Genesis 41:33–57). How was Joseph's admin-istrative ability demonstrated? Give specific examples.

Problem Solver.

The Apprentice

Q It was obvious to Pharaoh, an unbeliever, that Joseph had *'the spirit of God'* (Genesis 41:38). Why is this phrase important?

Q Do you, like Joseph, demonstrate to unbelievers that you have the Spirit of God within you? Do your friends, neighbours, or work col-leagues know you are a Christian? Are they able to see the difference this makes to the way you live? If your answer to one or more of these questions is 'no', *take time now* to bring this matter to the Lord and ask him to help you to rely each day on the power of the Holy Spirit to make you strong for him in front of others.

Another biblical example of the gift of administration in action is in Acts 6:1–7. The apostles' number one priority was preaching and teaching God's Word, yet there was a need for the local food programme to be properly administered.

Q From verse 3, what qualifications were necessary to organise this programme?

Q Do you think the apostles' priorities were right? (See verse 4.) What lessons do you learn from this about responsibility in the church?

Q How might the spiritual gift of administration be demonstrated in your church?

Q What should be your response towards those who clearly have this gift?

For private reflection:

◆ Do I set goals and identify the most efficient way to realise them?

◆ Do I cope well with multiple responsibilities in the process of achieving these goals?

◆ Do I have the ability to look ahead and troubleshoot potential areas of difficulty when I'm involved in a project?

◆ Do I organise people and events so that optimal results follow?

◆ Do I practise the principles of 1 Corinthians 13?

Do you think you might have the spiritual gift of administration?

Gift of leadership

Wise leaders are rare … They are able to see the big picture that often escapes those directly involved, so they make good mediators, advisers, and planners. Deborah fit this description perfectly. She had all these leadership skills, and she had a remarkable relationship with God … She didn't deny or resist her position in the culture as a woman and wife, but she never allowed herself to be hindered by it either. Her story shows that God can accomplish great things through people who are willing to be led by him.
Life Application Study Bible 4

'We have different gifts, according to the grace given us … if it is leadership, let him govern diligently …' (Romans 12:6,8).

Kise *et al* write that *'a person with the gift of leadership has the ability to motivate, coordinate, and direct the efforts of others in doing God's work'*.5 This gift shouldn't be confused with the gift of administration. While the gift of administration looks for ways in which goals can be carried out, those with the gift of leadership inspire vision by setting these goals in the first place and then communicating them to others. In addition, they have the God-given ability to motivate people to work together as they seek to carry out God's purposes. A clear example of the gift of leadership can be seen in the account of Deborah in Judges chapters 4 and 5. It's an important principle that leaders who want to be effective in God's service must first allow themselves to be led by God.

Read Judges 4,5

Q In chapter 4 verses 4–14, what evidence is there that Deborah was led by God?

Q What characteristics of leadership can be seen in her life?

Read Luke 22:25,26; 1 Thessalonians 5:12,13; Hebrews 13:7

Q These verses give us further information about the characteristics of those with the gift of leadership. Make a list of these characteristics.

Speaks the word of God.   servant
Faithful   Young
Sets an example   Respected
Humble   Administer

Q Hebrews 13:17 tells us what our response should be to those who have the gift of leadership. According to this verse, what is the responsibility of leaders?

For private reflection:

◆ Do I encourage people to work towards 'the big picture'?

◆ Do I direct and motivate others to use their spiritual gifts?

◆ Do I have the courage to make unpopular as well as popular decisions?

◆ Do I acknowledge the biblical model of servant leadership?

◆ Do I practise the principles of 1 Corinthians 13?

Do you think that you might have the spiritual gift of leadership?

Part of leadership is assessing the character, skills, life experiences, temperament, personality, and spiritual gifts of each member of the team that are available to accomplish the task at hand. Then once people are assigned to appropriate responsibilities, watch out! People flourish when they're freed up to contribute to a plan's success.
Lynne and Bill Hybels [6]

Gift of apostleship

While the 'office' of apostle that the original disciples of Christ held is unique and no longer exists, the 'role' of apostle continues today and functions through the spiritual gift of apostleship.
Bruce Bugbee *et al* [7]

'But to each one of us grace has been given as Christ apportioned it ... It was he who gave some to be apostles ...' (Ephesians 4:7,11)

The Greek root of the word 'apostle' means 'sent out with a mission or a message'. The Latin root is 'missio', from where we get the word 'missionary'.

Q The twelve disciples of Jesus are sometimes referred to as apostles. Revelation 21:14 gives them a special place in the new Jerusalem. Why do you think they will be given this special honour?

The New Testament also includes other people as apostles, eg Barnabas and Paul (Acts 14:14); James (Galatians 1:19); Silas and Timothy (1 Thessalonians 1:1; 2:6). The New Testament apostles were unique in that they formulated Christian doctrine and laid foundations for the Christian church. However Kise *et al* refer to this gift as *'the ability to minister transculturally, starting new churches or ministries that impact multiple churches'*,[8] suggesting that the gift of apostleship still exists today. This would probably involve bringing the gospel to those who've never heard it, either at home or abroad, and may be paired with the gift of evangelism.

Although Paul was not one of the original twelve, his apostleship was recognised by the early church. We can learn a lot about him from the book of Acts as well as from the letters he sent to the various churches. The essential requirements for those with the gift of apostleship can be seen in his life.

Paul was sent with a mission

Read Acts 26:12–18

Q Who sent him and what was his mission?

Paul ministered across cultures

He went on three missionary journeys and details of the various places he visited are recorded in Acts: 13:1 – 14:28; 15:36 – 18:22; 18:23 – 21:16. Those who minister across cultures often have to travel extensively, but this might not always be necessary. Exercising the gift of apostleship might mean that someone builds up relationships with people who live locally but are of a different 'culture' in an attempt to bring God's Word to them. Give examples which would fit this category.

Paul started new churches

The first Christian church to be established in Europe was at Philippi during Paul's second missionary journey: Acts 16:11–40. It was suggested earlier that a person with the gift of apostleship might also have the gift of evangelism. In a modern-day church planting situation, how important is it for the apostle to have the gift of evangelism? Give a reason for your answer.

Paul had an impact on several churches

This can be seen from reading the letters which he sent to various groups of Christian believers. He sent letters to Christians at Rome, Corinth, Galatia, Ephesus, Philippi, Colossae and Thessalonica. What benefits result when a person with the gift of apostleship influences several churches?

Q What should be your response towards those who clearly have this gift?

For private reflection:

◆ Do I have a church base from which I could be sent out?

◆ Do I feel a compulsion to move into areas of service that involve crossing cultural boundaries, either in my own country or in some other?

◆ Do I have a desire to get involved in establishing churches where previously there were none?

◆ Do others in the church affirm my suitability for developing a new ministry elsewhere?

◆ Do I practise the principles of 1 Corinthians 13?

Do you think you might have the spiritual gift of apostleship?

> *Apostles who assume the difficult task of carrying the gospel across cultural barriers are greatly needed in our time. If the Christian church is to begin to keep pace with the mushrooming world population, it needs the ministry of those especially called and equipped to establish the Christian faith among new groups of people. Happily, God continues to raise up dedicated persons and to anoint them for this task. They deserve our respect and our support.*
> **Kenneth C Kinghorn** 9

Personal comment

A few months ago, one of our church members – let's call him Ron – had an idea. In fact, it was probably more than that; I think he had vision, one of the qualities of a real leader. He could see the possibilities, the potential and the power for good that could be unleashed if the local churches worked together to bring biblical truth to their neighbours in a way that they could understand – through video. The vision was cast and several church representatives met together regularly to pray for God's blessing on this new venture. Ron continued to contact other churches to invite them on board but it soon became clear that, although he could inspire and motivate people to rally to his call, he found it difficult to carry out the resulting administrative tasks satisfactorily. His burden was lifted, however, when one of the people from the other churches – Sandy – took on board the task of organising the administrative details. Sandy had the gift of administration! So Ron thankfully surrendered the organising to Sandy with his gift of administration and he, in turn, acknowledged with gladness that Ron had used his gift of leadership to cast the vision in the first place! Here was an example of the right people being in the right place for the right reason.

One of the books in the bibliography sounds pretty much like that. It's called Network: The Right People...In the Right Places...For the Right Reasons. *The authors believe that identifying your spiritual gift(s) is only part of a wider process. They suggest that, in order to play your part in the body of Christ in an effective, fulfilling way, you need to identify the elements which make up your 'servant profile'. These are passion ('where' you're motivated to serve); spiritual gifts ('what' you're equipped to do); and personal style ('how' you can best serve). Do you want to serve God as the right person in the right place for the right reason? Does he deserve anything less?*

4| Communicating God's Word

'And so we are continually thankful to God that when you heard the Word of God from us you accepted it, not as a mere human message, but as it really is, God's Word, a power in the lives of you who believe.'
1 Thessalonians 2:13 (Phillips Translation)

From what I see and sense in evangelical circles, I would have to say that about ninety percent of the religious work carried on in the churches is being done by ungifted members. I am speaking of men and women who know how to do many things but who fail to display the spiritual gifts promised through the Holy Spirit.
A W Tozer [1]

Have you ever come across newspaper headlines which have really made you laugh? Here are some examples: *'Two Sisters Reunited After 18 Years at Checkout Counter'; 'Local High School Dropouts Cut in Half'; 'Chef Throws His Heart into Helping Feed Needy'*.[2] These double-meaning headlines can be quite funny, can't they? Probably the journalist didn't realise their dual interpretation until after the newspaper had been printed – by then, it would be too late to rephrase. I think this highlights the importance of good communication – we can quite unintentionally convey the wrong meaning if we're not careful in our choice of words. God knows the importance of words and clear, correct communication. He chose to reveal the truth about himself through the words of the Bible and he uniquely gifts certain people with the ability to communicate the truth of these words through evangelism, prophecy and teaching.

The gift of evangelism

The Samaritans responded in large numbers ... In the middle of all this success and excitement, God directed Philip out to the desert for an appointment with an Ethiopian... Philip went immediately. His effectiveness in sharing the gospel with this man placed a Christian in a significant position in a distant country and may well have had an effect on an entire nation.
Life Application Study Bible [3]

'But to each one of us grace has been given as Christ apportioned it ... It was he who gave some to be ... evangelists ...' (Ephesians 4:7,11).

Leslie Flynn offers the following definition of the gift of evangelism: *'The gift of proclaiming the Good News of salvation effectively so that people respond to the claims of Christ in conversion and in discipleship'.*[4] The word 'evangelism' doesn't actually appear in the Bible – the nearest we get is the word 'evangelist' which comes from a Greek word meaning 'one who brings good news'. In Acts 21:8, Philip is called an evangelist. (This is the same Philip who had been one of the seven men chosen to administer the food programme in Acts 6:1–7.) In Philip's evangelistic ministry, we can see God working in a crowd and also in an individual.

Read Acts 8:5,6,12

Q Write down the main points of these verses.

Philip proclaimed the Good News about Jesus (verse 5); the crowds paid close attention to Philip's message (verse 6); and they believed and were baptised (verse 12).

Q What is your response to hearing about Jesus? Do you pay close atten-tion to what is said or do you listen half-heartedly? Have you believed in the truth of God's message of salvation or are you still undecided? You can't remain indifferent to the claims of Jesus Christ and his rele-vance to your life – *take time now* to ask the Lord to make you willing to give up everything which is displeasing to him and to place your faith in him alone for your salvation.

I think there can sometimes be a tendency to think of an evangelist as someone who speaks to massive crowds. This was certainly the case with Philip in Samaria, but an evangelist can also exercise his God-given ability on a one-to-one basis.

Read Acts 8:26–40

Q Philip was available for what God wanted him to do and he responded in obedience. Are you available for God to use you and work through you in the way he chooses? Are you prepared to be a witness for him, irrespective of whether he has given you the gift of evangelism? *Take time now* to ask the Lord to make you willing to do whatever task he has for you and trust him to equip you to carry it out.

Q In what ways did Philip use the Ethiopian treasurer's existing knowledge of the Bible as a springboard for sharing the good news about Jesus?

The incident of Philip and the Ethiopian treasurer shows the importance of 'meeting people where they are' as far as their understanding of biblical truth is concerned.

In the following examples, imagine that you have the gift of evangelism. How might you communicate the Good News by using this principle of 'meeting people where they are'?

◆ In discussion with a work colleague, you make reference to your church and its activities. Your colleague responds by saying that she only goes to church for weddings and funerals. She then asks you why you go to church.

◆ You're travelling alone by train and find yourself sitting next to a man who's reading a book. After a few minutes, he turns to you and says, 'Have you ever read this book? It shows that all faiths lead to God – it doesn't matter whether you're a Muslim, a Hindu, a Christian or a total unbeliever. God – if he exists at all – just wants you to be sincere.'

◆ You're about to settle a bill at the garage when you notice that the mechanic has undercharged you by £50. You point this out to him and he replies, 'Well, you've earned your ticket to heaven now!'

Well, how did you get on? Do you think you could translate your answers into a real life situation if necessary?

For private reflection:

◆ Do I have an overwhelming desire for people to come to know Jesus personally?

◆ Do I look for opportunities to share my faith with others?

◆ Do I feel relaxed when I talk to people about my personal relationship with Jesus?

◆ Do I show a sensitivity to others which influences the way I present the gospel to them?

◆ Do I practise the principles of 1 Corinthians 13?

Do you think you might have the spiritual gift of evangelism?

All Christians are called to be Christ's witnesses (Acts 1:8) ... Nevertheless, the gift of evangelism is given to some Christians to endow them with an unusual capacity to lead others into a saving relationship with Jesus Christ. The gift of evangelism is a special ability that helps one to bring the gospel with remarkable success to the unconverted.
Kenneth C Kinghorn [5]

The gift of prophecy

God no longer directly reveals 'new truth'; there is now a back cover to the Bible. The canon of Scripture is closed ... It is the work of the Holy Spirit to illumine the minds of those who are called to the prophetic office so they understand the Word of God and apply it with a depth impossible to those who do not have the gift of prophecy. It may sound like new truth freshly revealed – but to be biblical it must be based on the Word of God.
Billy Graham [6]

'And in the church God has appointed ... prophets ...' (1 Corinthians 12:28).

It's interesting to note that the gifts of prophecy and teaching are mentioned in all three New Testament lists of spiritual gifts. Bugbee *et al* suggest that *'prophecy is the divine enablement to reveal truth and proclaim it in a timely and relevant manner for understanding, correction, repentance, or edification'.*[7] The root meaning of prophecy is 'to speak forth' or 'to speak for another'. A great prophet in the Bible was John the Baptist. His main responsibility was to announce the start of Jesus' ministry, and to preach a message of repentance.

Read Luke 3:2–20

Q In the following table, match up the verses with the appropriate statements. (The statements are taken from the New International Version of the Bible.)

Luke	Statements
3:2	Produce fruit in keeping with repentance 3
3:3	The Word of God came to John 1
3:8	Herod ... locked John up in prison 7
3:16	One more powerful than I will come 4
3:18	John rebuked Herod 6
3:19	Preaching a baptism of repentance for the forgiveness of sins 2
3:20	John exhorted the people and preached the good news to them 5

(handwritten numbers in left margin: 1, 2, 3, 4, 5, 6, 7)

Prophets are rarely popular people because they often say things their listeners don't want to hear. This was certainly true of John who challenged King Herod to his face about his sin of adultery and ended up in prison as a result.

Read Matthew 11:2,3

Q John doubted whether Jesus was really the promised Saviour. What did he do about his doubts? What do you learn from this?

Are circumstances causing you to doubt your part in God's plan of things? Do you think he's made a mistake somewhere? At such times, do what John the Baptist did – turn to the One who can give you the assurance you need.

Read 1 Corinthians 14:1,3,4,31

Q Paul encourages the Corinthian believers to desire the gift of prophecy and states the purpose of this gift. What are the benefits which other believers will receive when the gift of prophecy is properly exercised?

The Bible warns us that not all prophecy comes from God (1 John 4:1).

There are such people as false prophets.

Read Matthew 7:15; Mark 13:22–23

Q What do these verses say about false prophets?

Q What steps can you take to prevent being deceived by false prophets?

For private reflection:

◆ Do I give more importance to the presentation of biblical truth than to my own personal comfort?

◆ Do I challenge people to respond to the truth of God's Word?

◆ Do I have the ability to apply biblical truth in a way that is relevant to contemporary situations?

◆ Do I warn unrepentant people of God's judgement on sin?

◆ Do I practise the principles of 1 Corinthians 13?

Do you think you might have the gift of prophecy?

The gift of teaching

Under the instruction of Priscilla and Aquila, Apollos became an able pastor to whom Paul could entrust one of the most critical church situations at the time. For all practical purposes, Priscilla and Aquila acted as a seminary faculty for a promising male pastoral student. They taught him those redemptive events of the life of Christ about which he had been left uninformed along with their theological significance, and they gave him the overview of Christian doc-

trine that is suggested by the expression 'the way of God' (Acts 18:26). Paul and the churches reaped the benefits of their teachings through the ministry of Apollos.
Gilbert Bilezikian 8

'We have different gifts, according to the grace given us ... if it is teaching, let him teach ...' (Romans 12:6,7).

Like the gift of prophecy, the gift of teaching is mentioned in the three main New Testament lists of spiritual gifts. Bugbee *et al* describe the gift of teaching as *'the divine enablement to understand, clearly explain, and apply the word of God, causing greater Christ-likeness in the lives of listeners'.*9 This description would probably be true of Priscilla and Aquila, the husband-and-wife team who taught Apollos, the travelling preacher.

Read Acts 18:1–3, 18,19; 24–26

Q What precisely did Priscilla and Aquila do in verse 26?

Q What important principles do you learn from this?

Q Give some examples of different ways in which people could use their gift of teaching to make a lasting contribution to the lives of other believers.

For private reflection:

◆ Do I enjoy spending time studying God's word?

◆ Do I have the ability to clearly communicate biblical principles to others?

◆ Do I present God's truth in a way that leads to life-change?

◆ Do others say I help them to understand the Bible better?

◆ Do I practise the principles of 1 Corinthians 13?

Do you think you might have the gift of teaching?

Personal comment

I'm convinced I don't have the gift of evangelism. Whenever I meet someone who makes a comment about the church or religion or the meaninglessness of life (among other things), I take so long to think up a suitable response that the moment passes and the opportunity to speak for the Lord is gone. Ever been there? Yet some Christians revel in these kinds of opportunities and just can't get enough of them. There's a reason for that, of course – they're spiritually gifted to be evangelists. So, does this let the rest of us off the hook? I don't think so because in Acts 1:8, the risen Lord says to his followers: 'But you will receive power when the Holy Spirit comes on you; and you will be my witnesses in Jerusalem, and in all Judea and Samaria, and to the ends of the earth.' Can we still be witnesses for Jesus if we don't have the gift of evangelism? I'm sure the answer to that has to be 'yes'. A witness is someone who tells what he or she has seen. We don't need to think up clever answers to people's comments – but we do need to rely on the power of the Holy Spirit to give us the right words to say to those we meet who don't yet believe in our Lord Jesus.

In 1 Peter 3:15, we read, 'Always be prepared to give an answer to everyone who asks you to give the reason for the hope that you have.' This verse isn't addressed just to evangelists – all Christians need to take heed of it! Are you prepared to give an answer? If not, how do you become prepared? One way is to think of the various questions people might ask. Why are you opposed to abortion? Would you know what to say if someone asked you? Or someone might notice you stay positive at work when all around you are grumbling and complaining. Would you be prepared to give an answer if they asked you the reason why you're like that? Would you use the opportunity to say a word for the Lord, or would you let it go with some reference to the fact that it's just because you've got a sunny nature? Peter goes on in the same verse to say, 'But do this (give an answer) with gentleness and respect' (parenthesis added). Perhaps if we paid more attention to this part of the verse, people might be more interested in listening to what we have to say ...

Even if we don't have the gift of evangelism, we don't need to be afraid of evangelising. A very helpful book for those of us who tend to be a bit scared in this area is How To Talk About Jesus Without Freaking Out *by Jim/Karen Covell and Victorya Michaels Rogers.*[10] *The authors have spent several years teaching Christians who work in the entertainment industry in Hollywood – very likely one of the most difficult places in which to share your faith! I suggest you read this book – who knows, you might even end up discovering a gift you thought you didn't have!*

5| Understanding God's ways

'My prayer for you is that you may have still more love – a love that is full of knowledge and every wise insight. I want you to be able always to recognise the highest and the best, and to live sincere and blameless lives until the day of Christ.'
Philippians 1:9,10 (Phillips Translation)

I'm willing to have you call me for whatever you have created me to be and I come back to this theme – you designed me, you gifted me, to match up to what you've designed me to do. My gifting, my calling, matches up to the plan and purpose you have for my life.
Jill Briscoe [1]

Have you ever spent time studying for an exam? If so, you'll know only too well what it's like to sit for hours on end in front of mountains of books and papers. You've probably thought that your brain would explode if it had to take in any more information! Then there's the fear of forgetting what you've learned – what if you can't remember it on the day? Or what if you have to present the information in a way that differs from the way you've learned it? These are real anxieties for the serious student! However, I've found that if students *understand* something of what they're learning, then they're in a much better position to remember their material and to give satisfactory answers in the exam. When we consider the gifts of wisdom, knowledge and discernment, we too are brought into the realm of understanding – understanding God's ways.

The gift of wisdom

Those who have the gift of wisdom know how to get to the heart of a problem quickly. They have practical minds and are problem solvers. They have little difficulty in making decisions because they can foresee with a fairly high degree of accuracy what the outcome of the decisions will be. When those with the gift of wisdom speak, other members of the Body recognise that truth has been spoken and the right course of action recommended.
C Peter Wagner [2]

'To one there is given through the Spirit the message of wisdom ...' (1 Corinthians 12:8).

According to Kenneth Kinghorn, this spiritual gift *'is a special power given only to some Christians, enabling them to apply spiritual truth to a specific issue in an especially relevant fashion'* [3] James, the half-brother of Jesus, is a good example of one who applied the message of wisdom to a specific issue. Acts 15 describes the first church conference which took place. Here, the issue in question was discussed and, in response to James' message of wisdom, a decision was implemented. Using part of Kinghorn's definition suggested above, answer the following questions:

Q What was the specific issue involved? (Acts 15:1)

Q How did James apply spiritual truth? (15:13–21)

Q In what way was his application of spiritual truth especially relevant?

Q What was the outcome? (15:22–31)

The spiritual gift of the *message of wisdom* isn't given to every Christian. However, the Bible encourages all believers to possess wisdom.

Match up the verses below with the appropriate commands.

Verses	Commands about wisdom
Psalm 90:12	Get wisdom
Proverbs 4:5	Know wisdom
Proverbs 29:3	Act in wisdom
Ecclesiastes 8:16	Love wisdom
Colossians 4:5	Ask for wisdom
James 1:5	Gain a heart of wisdom

For private reflection:

◆ Do I have a desire for God's wisdom to guide my decisions?

◆ Do I have the ability to recognise solutions to complex problems?

◆ Do I give clear advice when others are in difficulty?

◆ Do others think of me as a wise person?

◆ Do I practise the principles of 1 Corinthians 13?

Do you think you might have the spiritual gift of the message of wisdom?

The gift of knowledge

This act (Ananias and Sapphira's sin) was judged harshly because dishonesty, greed, and covetousness are destructive in a church, preventing the Holy Spirit from working effectively. All lying is bad, but when we lie to try to deceive God and his people about our relationship with him, we destroy our testimony for Christ.
Life Application Study Bible 4

'... to another the message of knowledge ...' (1 Corinthians 12:8).

One definition of the spiritual gift of the message of knowledge is the

God-given *'ability to understand truth that is unknown by natural means'.*[5.] An example of this gift in action can be seen in the account of Peter's response to Ananias and Sapphira.

Read Acts 5:1–11

Q In your own words, summarise the story.

Q What was the specific sin that Ananias and Sapphira had committed?

Q If Peter had *not* applied the message of knowledge at this particular time, what might have been the effects on the church?

Q The insight which Peter showed can't be separated from his understanding of the scriptures (see Acts 2:14–41) and his close relationship with the Lord. Why is it important that a person gifted with the message of knowledge should have a thorough understanding of biblical truth?

Q What principles need to be kept in mind when using and/or witnessing this gift? (The following references might help you in answering this question: Acts 17:11; 1 Corinthians 8:1; 16:14; 2 Corinthians 11:13–15.)

Having knowledge of biblical truth isn't restricted only to those with the spiritual gift of the *message of knowledge*. In fact, it was the apostle Paul's desire that the Christians to whom he wrote would receive knowledge.

Read Philippians 1:9–11; Colossians 1:9–12

Q What does Paul say about this in his prayers?

Choose a Christian known to you for whom you will pray one of the above prayers. Do this on a regular basis and let them know you're praying for them in this way.

For private reflection:

◆ Do I have a desire to really understand biblical truths?

◆ Do I search the scriptures for insight and understanding?

◆ Do I help others to understand God's Word?

◆ Do I have an unusual insight or understanding which is helpful to my church or fellowship?

◆ Do I practise the principles of 1 Corinthians 13?

Do you think you might have the spiritual gift of the message of knowledge?

While this is a real gift, it is also easy to abuse. Someone who claims to have the gift might 'reveal' something that is not from God at all. Or someone might make up something to give credibility to his or her ministry. If you think you possess this gift be very cautious how freely you use it. The negative impact on individuals to whom you give incorrect information can be enormous.
Discipleship Journal 6

The gift of distinguishing between spirits

Without the gift of discernment operating in the church, the Christian community would be totally vulnerable. So long as falsehood and evil insinuate themselves into the life of the church, this gift provides an invaluable ministry among those who name Jesus as Lord.
Kenneth C Kinghorn [7]

'... to another distinguishing between spirits ...' (1 Corinthians 12:10).

This spiritual gift (also known as discernment) has been defined as *'the God-given ability to discern between truth and error, identifying deception or whether something is of God or not'.*[8] A very clear example of the gift of discernment in operation can be seen when the apostle Paul confronts the sorcerer and false prophet, Bar-Jesus, who was also known as Elymas.

Read Acts 13:6–12

Q Who was Bar-Jesus?

Q What was his initial response to Paul and Barnabas?

Q How was this demonstrated?

Q In your own words, summarise what Paul said to the sorcerer.

Q Give two outcomes resulting from this incident.

The Bible warns us of the existence of evil spirits who often appear in disguised form and, therefore, might not be readily recognised.

Read 2 Corinthians 11:14,15; 2 Thessalonians 2:9

Q What is the main point of each passage?

Q In light of the above, what does 1 John 4:1 urge us to do?

This indicates that, even if we don't have the spiritual gift of discernment, we still have a responsibility to test spiritual claims before we decide whether or not to trust them. Don't be a naïve Christian – not all that claims to be of God *is* of God. Counterfeit spiritual gifts really do exist (see Matthew 24:24).

For private reflection:

◆ Do I immediately detect error if it is present when I read or listen to religious material?

◆ Do I recognise whether or not a word which is said to come from God is authentic?

◆ Do I 'see through' other people's deception?

◆ Do I have a sense of evil if it is present?

◆ Do I practise the principles of 1 Corinthians 13?

Do you think you might have the spiritual gift of discernment?

Personal comment

Have you ever come across an illustration which really helps you to understand a particular principle? Some years ago, I heard someone tell the story of a bank clerk who was able to recognise forged bank notes. He was quick to spot these notes, even when the forgery took different forms. One of his friends asked him how much time he spent studying all the different types of forged notes and he replied that he didn't spend any time doing this. Puzzled, his friend then went on to ask how the bank clerk knew a forged note when he saw one. The clerk replied he familiarised himself with the genuine bank notes to such an extent that any note which deviated from this had to be a forgery. I think there's a valuable spiritual lesson here which ties in to what we've been studying in this chapter. Whenever someone in the church fellowship claims to give a message of knowledge, another with the spiritual gift of discernment will be able to pick up on the authenticity or otherwise of that message. This gift of discernment will serve the function of either validating the message or showing it up as being false. One way in which experts detect forged notes is by holding them up to the light. We too, irrespective of whether we have the gift of discernment, need to hold up everything that people say to the light of God's Word. No genuine message of knowledge or of wisdom will ever contradict what is said in the Bible. Remember that the Holy Spirit who gives these particular gifts is also the One who has authored the Bible and he is always in harmony with himself. So then, let's make sure we know the genuine article – God's Word – inside out, so we can discern between true and false teachings. Let's be glad that there are skilled bank clerks who can tell the difference between genuine and forged notes – similarly, we should be grateful to the Lord that he gives the gift of discernment to certain people in the church fellowship so that any message lacking the genuine stamp of God's Word and Spirit will be seen for what it is – false; while any message which is truly God-given will be embraced and acted on by the rest of the church.

6| Caring for God's people

'Share each other's troubles and problems, and in this way obey the law of Christ.'
Galatians 6:2 (NLT)

The church will begin to function more fully as God intended when spiritual gifts resume their rightful place within the life of the congregation. Spiritual gifts are given by God for a twofold purpose – to build up the body of Christ and to equip it for ministry (Ephesians 4:12). When the spiritual gifts function properly in the church we have a much better prospect of fulfilling the prayer that Jesus taught His disciples – 'Thy kingdom come, Thy will be done on earth as it is in heaven' (Matthew 6:10).
Kenneth C Kinghorn [1]

It's amazing the things which stick in your memory, isn't it? I remember some years ago teaching a class of students who had a very special relationship with each other. If one of them was feeling out of sorts, the others would show their concern by saying something encouraging. If another was going through a particularly bad time, the others would rally round and do what they could to support that student. In short, these students cared for each other – and it showed. God believes that caring is of such importance that he gave certain people special abilities to care for others in the church fellowship. I've certainly been glad of those gifted people who've encouraged me to persevere when I've felt like quitting; I've been thankful to those who've 'gone the extra mile' by exercising their gift of mercy; and I've known the security of being pastored by a shepherd who cared for the people in his church.

The gift of encouragement

Encouragement is not doing for someone what they can do for them-
selves. It is not removing pain from their lives. It is noticing them,
feeling with them, and reminding them of the hope we have in
Christ as we persevere in our walk with Him.
Lois Mowday Rabey [2]

'We have different gifts, according to the grace given us. If a (person's) gift is … encouraging, let him encourage …' (Romans 12:6,8).

Phyllis Bennett defines the spiritual gift of encouragement as *'the God-given ability to affirm, build up, or reassure those who are discouraged, weakening in their faith, or need affirmation for their usefulness to others'.*[3] The root word is 'advocate' or 'comforter' and is the same word that Jesus used to describe the Holy Spirit in John 14:16,26. This gift was so evident in the behaviour of one Bible character that the Christians in Jerusalem nicknamed him 'Barnabas', which means 'son of encouragement'. Barnabas demonstrates several different ways in which encouragement can be shown.

Read Acts 4:37; 9:26,27; 11:22–24; 15:36–40

Q What are the different ways in which Barnabas gives encouragement?

Q Regardless of whether you have the spiritual gift of encouragement, choose one of the above examples and say how you can apply it to your present circumstances.

Barnabas used his gift of encouragement in his relationships with both Paul and John Mark. With both men he took risks. In his initial encounter with Paul (Acts 9:26,27), Barnabas *risked his life* by offering to meet with such an unlikely convert. In being prepared to give John Mark a second chance (Acts 15:36–40), Barnabas *risked his friendship* with Paul.

Q What are some of the risks you might need to take as you encourage a Christian known to you?

Q Can you think of a situation in your own life when encouraging a Christian friend caused a strain or even a breakdown in your relationship with another Christian? Have you allowed this downturn in your relationship to continue? If so, *take time now* to consider what positive steps you'll take to try to restore your friendship with that person.

For private reflection:

◆ Do I take time to come alongside someone who needs to be encouraged?

◆ Do I challenge others to put their trust in God's promises?

◆ Do I have a desire for people to grow and develop in Christian faith and practice?

◆ Do others think of me as an encouraging person?

◆ Do I practise the principles of 1 Corinthians 13?

Do you think you might have the spiritual gift of encouragement?

The gift of mercy

Every Christian is expected to be merciful. This is a role that reflects the fruit of the Spirit. But those who have the gift of mercy make compassion and kindness their lifestyle. They do not simply react to emergencies, as every Christian is supposed to do. They continually seek opportunities to show pity for the miserable.
C Peter Wagner [4]

'We have different gifts according to the grace given us. If a (person's) gift is ... showing mercy, let him do it cheerfully' (Romans 12:6,8).

Peter Wagner suggests that *the gift of mercy is the special ability that God gives to certain members of the Body of Christ to feel genuine empathy and compassion for individuals, both Christian and non-Christian, who suffer distressing physical, mental or emotional problems, and to translate that compassion into cheerfully done deeds that reflect Christ's love and alleviate the suffering*.5 The main difference between this and the previous gift we studied is that the gift of encouragement operates mainly through loving words, while the gift of mercy operates through loving actions. A good example of this gift in action is the story of the Good Samaritan.

Read Luke 10:25–37

Q Write down specific ways in which the Samaritan showed mercy to the injured man.

Several verses in the Bible teach about the importance of showing mercy.

Read Matthew 5:7; 10:42; 25:31–40

Q Write down what you learn from each verse.

The spiritual gift of mercy is more than natural human sympathy or kindness – it is a special ability given by God for reaching out to those who hurt and are in need. The Lord is concerned that those who exercise this gift do so in the right spirit – Romans 12:8 reminds us that mercy should be shown with cheerfulness.

Q Why is this important?

Q Even if you don't have the spiritual gift of mercy, do you think it's a quality that all Christians should display in some form? Give a reason for your answer.

Q Make a list of specific ways in which you could enrich your church fellowship by acts of mercy.

Are you prepared to act on these ideas in the above list or are they going to remain theoretical possibilities? Take time now to seriously consider what you believe the Lord wants you to do about this. Ask him to help you to respond in obedience to whatever he says.

For private reflection:

◆ Do I know the love of God in my own experience to such an extent that I want to reach out to others who are in trouble?

◆ Do I see each life as one that matters to God?

◆ Do I gladly show compassion to those in need?

◆ Do I appreciate the need to set boundaries when showing mercy so that people will not become too dependent on me?

◆ Do I practise the principles of 1 Corinthians 13?

Do you think you might have the spiritual gift of mercy?

The gift of pastoring

I believe that thousands of Christians throughout the world who will never become pastors of churches do have the gift of a pastor that can be used to assist the clergy in their work. Those who have the gift should use it as fully as possible, remembering that failure to do so is

to grieve the Holy Spirit. Many pastors of churches are overworked and could use a little help. Each of us might well ask his pastor what to do to help him.
Billy Graham 6

'It was he who gave some to be ... pastors' (Ephesians 4:11).

The spiritual gift of pastoring or shepherding enables a person *'to guide and care for other Christians as they experience spiritual growth'.*7 The supreme example of pastoring is the Lord Jesus Christ – referred to in Hebrews 13:20 as 'that great Shepherd of the sheep'. Throughout the three years he spent with his disciples, Jesus clearly showed what it means to guide and care for Christians so that they will grow spiritually. At least three principles of pastoring can be seen in his life.

First, he guided those in his care as he led by example. In the table below, match up the verses with the appropriate examples.

Verses	Ways in which Jesus led by example
Matt 6:5–15	Showed compassion to the guilty
Luke 8:43–48	Servant leadership
John 8:1–11	Taught his disciples to pray
John 14:2–5;15–17	Made time for the needy

Secondly, he nurtured his followers by feeding them the Word of God. In Matthew 5, from verse 21 to the end of the chapter, Jesus referred to Old Testament commands concerning murder, adultery, divorce, oaths, revenge and how to respond to enemies.

Read Matthew 5:21–48

Q Choose one of these commands and write down how Jesus extended its application. How might someone with the gift of pastoring use the verse which you have chosen in a contemporary situation?

Thirdly, he protected his disciples from danger.

Read Luke 8:22–25; 22:31,32; John 18:8,9

Q Which specific dangers did Jesus protect his disciples from?

You don't have to be a pastor to have the gift of pastoring – when gifted Christians use this gift to respond to others in the church fellowship, an enormous burden is lifted from the official pastor or minister.

Q How might someone with the gift of pastoring minister to one of the following?

◆ A young person who is beginning to lose interest in Christian activities

◆ A person who has recently become a Christian

◆ A single mother who has difficulties with her children

◆ A man in your church fellowship who is addicted to pornography

◆ The people in your Bible study group

◆ An overseas student who is very homesick

For private reflection:

◆ Do I have a desire to guide, feed and protect a group of people in my church fellowship over a period of time?

◆ Do I have a concern for people who are beginning to drift away from Christian principles?

◆ Do I model, on a daily basis, what it means to follow the Lord wholeheartedly?

◆ Do I have the trust and confidence of others in the church?

◆ Do I practise the principles of 1 Corinthians 13?

Do you think you might have the spiritual gift of pastoring?

Personal comment

Let me ask you a question – how important do you think it is to care for your family? I imagine you would think it's pretty important. Here's another question – how important do you think it is to care for people in God's family ie those in your church fellowship? I can almost hear some of you saying 'Well, it's important, but that's the pastor's job'; or 'I suppose it's of some importance, but surely it's much less important than teaching or evangelism?' Well, there's no suggestion in the Bible that caring for God's people should be limited only to one person in the church or that it should be low down in our list of priorities. In fact, in John 13:35, Jesus says to his close followers: 'Your love for one another will prove to the world that you are my disciples' (NLT). Yet, so often, Christians neglect the spiritual gifts involved in caring for our brothers and sisters in the Lord. These gifts – encouragement, mercy and pastoring – are vital to a church fellowship if it is to function effectively as a community of believers. Take, for example, the gift of encouragement. Have you ever started a project – DIY at home, or taken lessons to learn a musical instrument? It can be quite tough to begin with, can't it? Many people have been on the verge of giving up – but someone took the time to encourage them to persevere. Hebrews 10:24 talks about spurring one another on, and the next verse specifically mentions encouraging one another. Encouragement has to be verbal. This means it's not enough just to think encouraging thoughts about people – we need to communicate these thoughts to them and to show them how far they've made progress as Christians, even though they might still have a long way to go. A simple 'You're doing well' can work wonders. Encouragement also promotes spiritual growth. When someone encourages us to carry on, we end up reaching goals that we never thought we'd meet. I think that every church fellowship needs several people with the caring gifts – I doubt if we could ever have too much encouragement, mercy or pastoring! What do you think?

7| Supporting God's people

'You must each make up your own mind as to how much you should give. Don't give reluctantly or in response to pressure. For God loves the person who gives cheerfully. And God will generously provide all you need. Then you will always have everything you need and plenty left over to share with others.'

2 Corinthians 9:7,8 (NLT)

Beware the darkness of the limelight. Be faithful to the calling and ministry God has given you, knowing that Christ, who sees and appreciates your every service to Him, is with you wherever you are – whether others recognize it or not.

Steven C Lombardo [1]

'I just can't make it on my own!' she cried. Recently widowed, Michelle was finding it hard to carry on. Friends rallied round to offer financial help, a listening ear, child-minding help – they wanted to support Michelle through this difficult new life which had thrust itself upon her. They did all this because they loved her. Part of Ephesians 5:25 says that the Lord 'loved the church and gave himself up for her'. Do *we* love the church and the people in it? Are we prepared to give ourselves up for other Christians who need our support? Even if we don't have the spiritual gifts of giving, helping and service, we can't opt out of supporting one another in our church fellowship. And for those of you who do have one or more of these gifts, have you recognised this yet and are you developing the gift(s) in ways which make a practical difference to other Christians? I hope this chapter will help you on your way!

The gift of giving

We must also remember that what we give – the amount or value – isn't as important as the attitude with which it is given. Our gifts should reflect an attitude of love. Am I a willing, cheerful giver? Or do I give out of a sense of obligation? When God places a specific need on our heart, we should supply that need, 'not reluctantly or under compulsion, for God loves a cheerful giver' (2 Corinthians 9:7).

Gracie Malone [2]

'We have different gifts according to the grace given us. If a (person's) gift is … contributing to the needs of others, let him give generously …' (Romans 12:6,8).

I was struck by this description of the gift of giving: *'The gift of giving is the divine enablement to contribute money and resources to the work of the Lord with cheerfulness and liberality. People with this gift do not ask "How much money do I need to give to God?" but, "How much money do I need to live on?"'*[3] A good example of this gift in operation is the generosity of the churches in Macedonia – Philippi, Thessalonica, and Berea – in supporting the Christians in Jerusalem during the apostle Paul's third missionary journey.

Read 2 Corinthians 8:1–5

Q Were the Macedonian Christians wealthy? (verse 2)

Q What does this tell you about the relationship between wealth and the gift of giving?

Q How much did these people give? (verse 3)

Q How would you describe their attitude? (verse 4)

Q In addition to material giving, the Macedonian Christians *'gave them-selves first to the Lord ...'* (verse 5). Why is this important?

The Bible gives us various principles when it comes to how we should give. In the table below, match up the verses with the correct examples of ways which should govern our giving.

Verses	How we should give
Matthew 5:42	Give quietly
Matthew 6:3,4	Give sacrificially
Luke 21:1–4	Give cheerfully
2 Corinthians 8:7	Give when requested
2 Corinthians 9:2	Give excellently
2 Corinthians 9:7	Give readily

Is the Lord challenging you about some aspect of your giving eg your attitude, the amount you give, the people you give to (or don't give to)? *Take time now* to let the Lord examine your thoughts about giving and be prepared for him to direct you to make changes in this regard.

For private reflection:

◆ Do I manage my finances and my lifestyle in such a way that giving to the Lord's work is top priority?

◆ Do I make a habit of giving generously, cheerfully, and sacrificially?

◆ Do I have a desire that my giving will promote spiritual development in others?

◆ Do I trust God to provide for me whenever I give to others?

◆ Do I practise the principles of 1 Corinthians 13?

Do you think you might have the spiritual gift of giving?

The gift of helping

The person with the gift of helping is often a background person who makes things happen without being noticed. Even though this gift is often overlooked, it is a vital act of ministry in the Christian church.
Jim Burns and Doug Fields [4]

'And in the church God has appointed ... those able to help others ...'
(1 Corinthians 12:28).

Helping is an important, and often undervalued, spiritual gift which comes from a Greek word meaning 'support'. One set of authors suggests that *'a person with the gift of helping has the ability to work alongside others and attaches spiritual value to the accomplishment of practical and often behind-the-scenes tasks that sustain the Body of Christ'.*[5] A Christian in the Bible who probably had the gift of helping was Phoebe.

Read Romans 16:1,2

Q How is she described? (verse 1)

Q Why did Paul ask the Christians in Rome to give her any help she might need? (verse 2)

Q Phoebe helped 'many people' (verse 2). What does this suggest about the frequency with which she used her gift?

Q Paul states that Phoebe was also a help to him (verse 2). In what way(s) might she have helped him?

The gift of helping is mainly to 'free up' other Christians so they can serve God by using the spiritual gifts he has given to them. It involves the idea of removing burdens from people's shoulders in order for them to be more effective in the work of the Lord.

Q Make a list of specific ways in which someone with the gift of helping could support others in their church fellowship.

The gift of helping is not usually a public one like the gifts of teaching or evangelism or prophecy, for example. Nevertheless, it is an indispensable gift in any church fellowship and there are probably several Christians in a local fellowship who have this gift. However, the person with the gift of helping also needs to receive from others.

Q Can you think of a way in which someone might minister to a person who has the gift of helping?

For private reflection:

◆ Do I take delight in working behind the scenes, even though what I do might not be noticed by others?

◆ Do I enjoy doing practical tasks which support others in their work for the Lord?

◆ Do I recognise the spiritual importance of helping others?

◆ Do I receive satisfaction from doing jobs that others might consider 'menial'?

◆ Do I practise the principles of 1 Corinthians 13?

Do you think you might have the spiritual gift of helping?

The spiritual gift of serving

Keep in mind ... that being a servant does not mean doing a few good things for people. It means a way of living *that God has chosen for us and demonstrated for us in Christ. Jesus was called to serve, and he did. We are called to serve, and we must.*
Ray Hoo [6]

'We have different gifts, according to the grace given us. If a (person's) gift is ... serving, let him serve' (Romans 12:6,7).

Peter Wagner suggests that *'the gift of service is the special ability that God gives to certain members of the Body of Christ to identify the unmet needs involved in a task related to God's work, and to make use of available resources to meet those needs and help accomplish the desired goals'.*[7]

Read 1 Corinthians 16:15–18

Q Stephanas and others 'devoted themselves to the service of the saints' (verse 15). In verse 16, what instruction is given to Christians regarding their appropriate response to people like Stephanas?

Q Why is this an important principle in the life of the church?

Q A phrase in verse 17 is 'they have supplied what was lacking from you'. How does this relate to what Peter Wagner says about identifying unmet needs? (See his definition of the gift of serving.)

Q Why is it important that other Christians make up for what we lack in terms of spiritual gifts?

Those with the gift of serving get involved in things that others would shy away from.

Read John 13:1–17

Q Jesus gives a tremendous example of serving in action. What important principles of serving can you find in this account?

Q Make a list of examples of how people can serve in the church. Be as specific as you can.

Q What would be the consequences if no one served in the ways you listed above?

Q What does this tell you about the gift of serving?

Examine your attitudes towards serving. Do you see yourself as the servant of others in your church fellowship? Is your attitude the same as Jesus who *'made himself nothing, taking the very nature of a servant ...'* (Philippians 2:7)? *Take time now* to ask the Lord to bring your attitudes into line with his.

For personal reflection:

◆ Do I have the ability to identify what needs to be done in a given situation to further God's work?

◆ Do I have the willingness to put others' needs before my own in order for the work of the Lord to grow?

◆ Do I offer my skills to assist what is going on in my church fellowship?

◆ Do others rely on my support?

◆ Do I practise the principles of 1 Corinthians 13?

Do you think you might have the gift of serving?

Personal comment

There are some spiritual gifts where we just don't get a look in, aren't there? For example, not every Christian is a teacher or administrator or leader, and those without these gifts would do well to leave these responsibilities to those who have! Yet, quite a lot of the gifts seem to extend beyond our specific areas of giftedness. The ones in this chapter are examples of this – you may not have the spiritual gift of giving, but does that mean you're exempt from giving any of your resources to the work of the Lord? Perhaps you don't have the spiritual gift of helping, but does that mean you take a hands-off approach when a Christian needs some assistance? Or maybe you don't have the gift of serving – that's somebody else's job, so you think it doesn't concern you. Well, there's no denying that the Spirit gives gifts of giving, helping and serving to specific individuals in the church. However, that doesn't let the rest of us off the hook – giving, helping and serving should be part-and-parcel of every Christian's contribution to the life and well-being of the body of Christ. Let's get specific: over the next few weeks, ask yourself how you can please the Lord by your giving. Do you give any money to your church fellowship? Do you give in proportion to your income? Do you give gladly and without complaining? Do you give even when it really costs you? What about giving other things, like time? How well do you manage this valuable resource? Is your life packed with so many activities that you think you just don't have time to give to a Christian in need? Do you use the fact that you're busy as an excuse? Then there's the area of helping – when was the last time you offered assistance to someone in your church so that they could get on with the job that God has called them to do? What could you do that would help to lift a burden of work from someone's shoulders? Are you willing to approach your church leadership and ask what you can do to help? Would you be happy to do what was suggested, or would you want to help only in a certain way? All Christians are called to be servants – Jesus is our great model for this. Are you concerned mainly with your own interests and having other people serve you? Do you 'consider others better than yourselves' and 'look not only to your own interests, but also to the interests of others' (Philippians 2:3,4)? Every spiritual gift – without exception – should be used in the service of others and in line with 1 Corinthians 13. How are you doing?

8| Demonstrating God's power

'But you will receive power when the Holy Spirit comes on you; and you will be my witnesses in Jerusalem, and in all Judea and Samaria, and to the ends of the earth.'

Acts 1:8

So how should we think about faith and miracles today? First we should have no interest in taking any glory away from our Saviour. Instead of complimenting our faith, saying that we can do anything if we just have enough faith may do an injustice to the earthly work of Jesus. Even to the apostles, to whom he had given special powers to launch his kingdom on earth, Jesus said, 'Do not rejoice that the spirits submit to you, but rejoice that your names are written in heaven' (Luke 10:20).

Brad Atkins [1]

Have you ever watched documentaries which showed the devastating effects of tornadoes? There was a series of programmes on television some time ago which gave awesome camera footage of buildings being destroyed and trees being ripped out by their roots and hurled through the air as a result of the incredible force of the tornado. These pictures were an amazing example of power. God demonstrates his power too in the lives of Christians. Sometimes, his power is largely unseen by others, like when he strengthens a Christian to stay strong in the face of a particular temptation. At other times, he shows his power more visibly. In this chapter, we're going to look at God's power through the spiritual gifts of faith, healing and miracles.

The gift of faith

Faith is not a means by which we coerce God to do something He never intended. Rather, it is resting secure in the nature of God, trusting the outcome of every situation to Him ... Faith contrived to manipulate a specific answer to a human need, without the foundation of accepting God's will as pre-eminent, is no faith at all.
Martha E Chamberlain [2]

'Now to each one the manifestation of the Spirit is given for the common good ... to another faith by the same Spirit ...' (1 Corinthians 12:7,9).

Leslie Flynn defines the gift of faith as *'a Spirit-given ability to see something that God wants done and to sustain unwavering confidence that God will do it regardless of seemingly insurmountable obstacles'.*[3] It's important to distinguish between the *grace* of faith which all Christians possess (Ephesians 2:8) and the *gift* of faith which only some Christians possess as a result of being gifted in this way by the Holy Spirit. A man who exercised extraordinary faith in the face of 'seemingly insurmountable obstacles' was Abraham (Genesis 12–25).

Read Hebrews 11:8–19

Q This passage summarises various incidents in Abraham's life of faith. How did Abraham exercise the gift of faith in the face of these obstacles?

Q From the above incidents, which one impresses you the most? Give a reason for your answer.

Q These examples from the life of Abraham show what an amazing confidence he had in God. Why do you think it's important for a person with the spiritual gift of faith to have this confidence in God?

Q The person with the gift of faith sharpens this gift through prayer and a close relationship with the Lord. Part of this relationship will involve asking for things in Jesus' name (see John 14:13,14). Using these verses to guide you, what do you think it means to ask in his name?

For private reflection:

◆ Do I long for my desires to be in line with God's will and purposes?

◆ Do I develop a close relationship with the Lord through prayer?

◆ Do I believe God's promises and act on them?

◆ Do I have absolute confidence in God's power even when I'm faced with obstacles which appear insurmountable?

◆ Do I practise the principles of 1 Corinthians 13?

Do you think you might have the spiritual gift of faith?

The gift(s) of healing

God's main purpose for the believer is to conform him to the image of Christ. Whether or not God heals depends on whether illness or recovery best contributes to that end. Thus, the gift of healing should not be exercised on the basis of the patient's faith but on the condition of the will of God.
Leslie B Flynn [4]

'... to another gifts of healing by that one Spirit ...' (1 Corinthians 12:9).

According to Bruce Bugbee *et al*, *'the gift of healing is the divine enablement to be God's means for restoring people to wholeness'.*[5] There are several instances of healing in the New Testament and many people believe that such healing (plus the other 'sign' gifts of miracles, tongues and interpretation of tongues) was to authenticate the divine message of the Lord, his disciples and others. The apostle Paul was one of the 'others' who had the spiritual gift of healing.

Read Acts 28:7–9

Q Summarise the contents of this passage.

Q However, Paul wasn't able to exercise the gift of healing in all circumstances (see 2 Timothy 4:20). What does this tell you about this gift?

Q In 2 Corinthians 12:7–10, we have the account of Paul's struggle with an unspecified weakness which he calls a 'thorn in the flesh'. There are times when God doesn't heal, even when asked. Why do you think healing isn't always God's priority for a hurting Christian?

In the Bible, we read of different types of healing. They seem to be physical; emotional; relational and spiritual.

Read Matthew 9:35; Luke 4:18; Philemon vs 10–17; 1 Peter 2:24

Q How do you think the gift of healing might be demonstrated in the above ways in the church today?

Q When you read or hear of the gift(s) of healing, what comes to your mind? Do you usually think only of physical healing? Have you ever considered that this might be too narrow a view? Take time now to ask the Lord to help you to understand the place of this gift in the church today.

For personal reflection:

◆ Do I see myself as an instrument through whom God's healing power can flow?

◆ Do I recognise that the gift of healing doesn't operate in every needy situation?

◆ Do I have a biblical understanding of the place of healing in the lives of Christians?

◆ Do I acknowledge that God alone is the healer and he is in complete control of consequences?

◆ Do I practise the principles of 1 Corinthians 13?

Do you think you might have the spiritual gift of healing?

There is little direct instruction about healing in the New Testament. While Jesus models a vibrant healing ministry for us, much is left as a mystery. Healing is best understood as just one more way God shows us His love. When healing is elevated above other spiritual gifts, God's love can get lost in the distraction. Those who are not healed may feel that God disapproves of them. A healing ministry can remain authentic by staying biblical, focusing on God as the healer, rather than on those who are doing the praying.
Jane A G Kise *et al* 6

The gift of miracles

Why do we not see the spectacular miracles today that we read about in the Bible? Are few such miracles occurring because our faith is small – or could it be that God does not will the spectacular right now? Could it be that signs and wonders were gifts particularly appropriate to the special circumstances of the early Church? I think so. And today when the gospel is proclaimed on the frontiers of the

> *Christian faith that approximate the first century situation, miracles*
> *still sometimes accompany the advance of the Gospel. As indicated by*
> *both the prophets Hosea and Joel, as we approach the end of the age*
> *we may expect miracles to increase.*
> Billy Graham [7]

'... to another miraculous powers ...' (1 Corinthians 12:10).

Phyllis Bennett suggests that the gift of miracles is *'the God-given ability to be used as God's instrument to appropriate an extraordinary amount of God's power in such a way that Christ is glorified and the message of the gospel is authenticated'.*[8] Both the Old and New Testaments of the Bible have numerous examples of miracles – both genuine, that is from God, and counterfeit, eg Pharaoh's magicians in Exodus 7:10–12. In looking for a Bible character who had the spiritual gift of miracles, I came across Paul.

Read Acts 19:11

This verse raises several questions.

Q Who actually did the miracles – God or Paul?

Q Your answer to the above question is important – why?

Q Why do you think these miracles took place? (See 2 Corinthians 12:12)

Q Acts 19:12 suggests that Paul probably wasn't even present when these miracles happened. What does this tell you about the role of the person who is gifted in this way?

Q Miraculous demonstrations of God's power rarely take the form of the miracles mentioned in verse 12, at least not in contemporary Western culture. Some Christians believe that we have become so 'scientific' and 'naturalistic' in our society that this hinders the dramatic demonstration of God's power. To what extent do you agree or disagree with this view?

Our enemy, Satan, hates it when Christians use their spiritual gifts to honour the Lord and to build up a group of believers. So, he loves to deceive and confuse people about the gifts of the Spirit. One way in which he does this is by hiding behind counterfeit miracles.

Read 2 Thessalonians 2:9

Q What do you learn from this verse?

One of the greatest miracles of all which takes place today, in all cultures, is the miracle of the new birth when a person who was previously disinterested in or even hostile to the gospel becomes a new creation in Christ (2 Corinthians 5:17). Share with your group how the Lord used someone to bring about this miracle in your life.

For personal reflection:

◆ Do I have the desire to be used as God's instrument in any way he chooses?

◆ Do I want people's focus to be on the Lord and not on me as I serve him?

◆ Do I know the reality of God's power in a special way as I minister to others?

◆ Do others see God's power at work through me?

◆ Do I practise the principles of 1 Corinthians 13?

Do you think you might have the spiritual gift of miracles?

Personal comment

This has been a particularly interesting chapter to research. The gifts of faith, healing and miracles seem to hang together somehow. In some ways, these are rather mysterious gifts and Christians have different views about their emphasis in modern-day life. In preparing to write about the gift of faith, I came across several references to George Müller, the man who cared for a total of 10,000 orphans in Bristol over a period of sixty years. Müller exercised his gift of faith as he prayed for God's provision for the needs of the children. He received amazing answers to his believing prayers as he first of all made sure that what he was doing coincided with the will of God. This gave him the courage to ask God, in faith, for all that was needed to care for the children in the orphanage. Not once did God let him down. The gift of faith has to be exercised in line with the will of God. The same is true of the gift(s) of healing. Not everyone who wants to be healed is healed. It's simply not true to say that people will be healed if only they have enough faith. Imagine the false guilt this lays on Christians who are not restored to wholeness in this life! We can't manipulate God – but we can surrender to his purposes for us. I believe his main purpose for Christians is that they'll 'be conformed to the likeness of his Son ...' (Romans 8:29). The Lord might achieve this best by healing ... or by not healing. Are you allowing him to make you more like Jesus, regardless of your circumstances? And miracles ... when was the last time God showed you a miracle? Can you not remember? Could it be that you're not seeing miracles because you're not expecting them any more? Do you think you might be looking for something spectacular when God might want to get your attention by working quietly, but no less powerfully, in your life? Do you pray for the miracle of conversion for your unbelieving spouse/friend/neighbour/child/parent? Do you believe God will intervene in a difficult situation to which you can see no satisfactory solution? Do you praise him for the miracle of a transformed life when someone genuinely gives their life over to the Lord? I believe in miracles because I believe in the God who makes them happen. What about you?

9| Speaking God's language

'I wish you all had the gift of speaking in tongues, but even more I wish you were all able to prophesy. For prophecy is a greater and more useful gift than speaking in tongues, unless someone interprets what you are saying so that the whole church can get some good out of it.'
1 Corinthians 14:5 (NLT)

In the New Testament, tongues serve as a means of worship as a person prays to God in an unknown language (1 Corinthians 14:2) ... The obvious purpose of interpretation is to turn the congregation's attention away from the one speaking in tongues and focus the worship of the congregation towards God. When tongues are used, the worship of God becomes possible only if the congregation understands the meaning of what has been uttered. Paul required an interpretation of tongues for every public use of this gift.
Kenneth C Kinghorn [1]

I think it's fair to say that probably the most contentious and misunderstood gifts of the Spirit are tongues and interpretation of tongues. Genuine Christian believers have real differences of opinion about the existence and role of tongues and interpretation in the church today. Some categorically state that these gifts were only for the first-century church and have no place in the twenty-first century church; others believe that these gifts continue to be given by the Spirit to build up the church in the present time. Another difficulty is in knowing exactly what the gifts of tongues and interpretation actually were in New Testament times – some claim tongues was a special prayer language; others suggest this gift gives the unique ability to minister in the language of a foreign country when this language would normally be unknown to the speaker. In this chapter, we'll look at the gifts of tongues and their interpretation as well as paying some attention to problems associated with them.

The gift of tongues

If tongues is the gift of the Holy Spirit, it cannot be divisive in itself. When those who speak in tongues misuse it so that it becomes divisive, it indicates a lack of love. And those who forbid it do the Church a disservice because they appear to contradict the teaching of the apostle Paul. Those believers who do speak in tongues and those who do not should love each other and work for the greater glory of God in the evangelization of the world, remembering one thing: those who do speak in tongues and those who do not will live with each other in the New Jerusalem.
Billy Graham [2]

'Now to each one the manifestation of the Spirit is given for the common good ... to another the ability to speak in different kinds of tongues ...' (1 Corinthians 12:7,10).

One definition of the spiritual gift of tongues is *'the God-given ability to speak in unintelligible languages in order to, through interpretation, edify the church'.*[3] Whatever your view of tongues-speaking in the church today, there's no getting away from the fact that this gift certainly operated in New Testament times. Once again, the apostle Paul provides us with an example of someone who had this gift (1 Corinthians 14:18).

Read 1 Corinthians 14

Q According to Paul, what is the main purpose of the spiritual gift of tongues?

Q How does praying in tongues differ from normal praying?

Q Why, in a church context, is it essential that tongues should be interpreted?

Q Paul wanted the church at Corinth to know that the gift of tongues was no greater than any other gift of the Spirit. What specific instructions does he give for how this gift should be exercised? (See verses 26–28,33,40.)

Q As a result of what you've learned in this study, has your thinking about speaking in different kinds of tongues been challenged? If so, how?

Regardless of your view of the gift of tongues, what is your *attitude* towards those who have a different perspective? Is your main goal to persuade other Christians to think the same way as you on this issue, or are you prepared to emphasise those elements of your faith which you have in common and not major on the differences? Are you willing to lovingly accept Christians with a different viewpoint from yours as your brothers and sisters in Christ? Will you allow any disagreements to spoil any fellowship which you might have with them? *Take time now* to ask the Lord to help you to develop the right attitude towards Christians who don't see things exactly the way you do.

For private reflection:

◆ Do I understand what was meant by speaking in different kinds of tongues in New Testament times?

◆ Do I understand what might be involved in speaking in different kinds of tongues in today's church?

◆ Do I view this as one of the lesser gifts?

◆ Do I desire to be totally open to the work of the Holy Spirit?

◆ Do I practise the principles of 1 Corinthians 13?

Do you think you might have the spiritual gift of speaking in different kinds of tongues?

The gift of interpretation of tongues

God does not send messages to the congregation through the gift of speaking in tongues. He gives messages through such gifts as prophecy and teaching. Therefore, tongues are to be directed to God, not man. Prayer, praise and thanksgiving (biblical uses for this gift) are addressed upward to God. Any interpretation which purports to be a message from God to man is, from the biblical standpoint, highly suspect. Any interpretation of a tongue, if it is to accord with scripture, should interpret the utterance in tongues in terms of a prayer or words of praise or thanksgiving to God.
Kenneth C Kinghorn 4

'Now to each one the manifestation of the Spirit is given for the common good ... and to still another the interpretation of tongues.' (1 Corinthians 12:7,10).

*'The gift of interpreting tongues is the ability to understand and communicate the meaning of an unknown language spoken by someone who has the gift of tongues'.*5 These two gifts go together – there's no point in publically speaking in tongues if no one can interpret, and the gift of interpretation is useless if no one speaks in tongues. As with the gift of tongues, Paul gives clear instructions regarding the use of interpretation.

Read 1 Corinthians 14:5, 27,28

Q Write down what is said in each case about this.

The gifts of tongues and interpretation of tongues might not always be given to the same person – see 1 Corinthians 12:10. However, in chapter 14 verse 13, those who speak in tongues are encouraged to pray for the ability to interpret what they've said. In the verses which follow, there seems to be three purposes involved in speaking in tongues – praise, prayer and thanksgiving.

Read 1 Corinthians 14:14–16

Q What purpose is given for speaking in tongues in each of these three verses?

Q In the above instances, what do you think is the purpose of the gift of interpretation?

For personal reflection:

◆ Do I believe in the continuation of all the gifts of the Spirit?

◆ Do I speak to God in an unknown language and understand what is being said?

◆ Do I understand what is being said when I hear another Christian speak to God in an unknown language?

◆ Do others look to me for interpretation?

◆ Do I practise the principles of 1 Corinthians 13?

Do you think you might have the spiritual gift of interpretation of tongues?

Some important conclusions

In my judgement the Bible says that any believer can enjoy the filling of the Holy Spirit and know His power even though he or she has not had any sign such as speaking in tongues. On the occasion of a particular infilling, tongues may be a sign God gives some, but I do not find it is a sign for all. I do think it is important, though, for each of us to hold our opinion without rancour and without breaking our bonds of fellowship in Jesus Christ. We worship the same Lord, and for this we are grateful.
Billy Graham 6

At the beginning of this chapter, I mentioned that tongues and their interpretation can be controversial subjects among Christians. Some of you doing this Bible study will have different views from others who are also doing the study. I think it's important to remember that the purpose of any spiritual gift is to build up or strengthen the church, not destroy or weaken it through bickering and disagreement. In writing to the Corinthian church, Paul was very much aware of how different emphases on the importance of some of the spiritual gifts could lead to friction and misunderstanding. The Christians in the church at Corinth were abusing the gift of tongues and needed to be instructed in its correct use. Let's look at some principles which we can take on board to help us develop a right perspective on the gift of tongues.

Q It's no accident that 1 Corinthians 13 – the love chapter – is positioned immediately after a general discussion about spiritual gifts and right before a more specific discussion of prophecy, tongues and orderly worship. Why is it important that love should be prominent in the exercising of these gifts?

Q The church in Corinth had problems. Several of its members were confused over moral issues and were spiritually immature. Their worship was disorderly as far as the Lord's Supper (chapter 11) and their use of spiritual gifts like tongues (chapter 14) were concerned. Against this background, what importance would you give to the gift of tongues which some of the Corinthian Christians clearly had?

Some people erroneously think that having the gift of tongues is a short-cut to spiritual maturity. However, I believe that God has given us at least four ways by which we can grow spiritually.

Read Acts 17:11; Ephesians 6:18; Hebrews 10:24,25; 1 John 1:9

Q What are the four ways in which we can grow spiritually?

The gifts of tongues and interpretation of tongues should always be seen in the context of the other spiritual gifts operating in the body of Christ, the church. These are not 'special' gifts which are given to ultra-favoured Christians – in fact, nowhere in the Bible are we encouraged to seek the gift of tongues. At the same time, however, we're told in 1 Corinthians 14:39 not to forbid speaking in tongues. Some writers have summed up New Testament teaching on the issue by coining the phrase 'seek not, forbid not'.

Q *In no more than twenty words*, to what extent do you think this phrase is an accurate summary of the biblical position on tongues?

Has there been anything in this chapter which has challenged your views of tongues and their interpretation? Whatever your answer, *take time now* to ask the Lord to guide your thinking about these gifts, so that your outlook will be in line with biblical principles.

Personal Comment

Many of today's godly, mature and useful Christians have never spoken in tongues. Likewise, as far as we know it wasn't the spiritual gift of historical Christians like Augustine, Calvin, Luther, Knox, Bunyan, Wesley, Spurgeon, or Moody. Like all the spiritual gifts, the gift of tongues isn't given to every Christian believer. Therefore, contrary to what some people say, it is not necessary to have this gift in order to be filled with the Spirit. Being filled with the Spirit is more to do with bearing the fruit of the Spirit (Galatians 5:22,23) rather than using the gifts of the Spirit. No matter what gifts we've been given, none of them are substitutes for a life which is lived out daily under the control of the Holy Spirit and in obedience to the Lord's commands and purposes.

Like other spiritual gifts, speaking in tongues can be counterfeited. There is a lot of documented evidence from trustworthy sources that tongues-speaking takes place in several non-Christian religions – certainly it isn't the spiritual gift of tongues which is present in such cases. Similarly, there are reports of 'ecstatic utterances' in situations where there is a high level of emotional arousal – such psychological origins don't equate to the gift of tongues either. However, if the Spirit chooses to give the gift of tongues to specific people in the church, the gift of interpretation will also be present (either in the same or different person) and the use of these gifts should follow the procedure set out by Paul in 1 Corinthians 14:26–28,33. The correctness of the interpretation can be verified by others in the church eg those who have the gifts of discernment or teaching. In this way, interpretation can be checked against biblical revelation.

Finally, all the gifts of the Spirit (including tongues and their interpretation) must be exercised in love (1 Corinthians 13) with the purpose of edifying the church and promoting unity among Christian believers. If using your spiritual gifts brings disharmony to the body of Christ, then watch out, because it means Satan has gained the upper hand. How important is love in your church fellowship?

10| Have you unwrapped your gift yet?

'When he ascended to the heights, he ... gave gifts to his people.'
Ephesians 4:8

At the end of the day, God will not ask you why you didn't lead someone else's life or invest someone else's gifts. He will not ask, 'What did you do with what you didn't have?' Though, he will ask, 'What did you do with what you had?'
John Ortberg [1]

Well, we've looked at the various spiritual gifts mentioned in the New Testament. This may or may not be an exhaustive list of gifts. Not everyone agrees on what the gifts are or indeed on how many there are. Nevertheless, the ones listed in chapter two of this study give us a starting point in discovering what our gifts might be. But how do we actually go about finding out what spiritual gift has been given to us? How do we develop it? Are other people's views of our gifts important? How does my gift fit in with the gifts of others in the church? In this final chapter, we're going to try to answer some of these questions but, first of all, we'll begin by reviewing previous chapters in this study. Are you ready? Then, let's go!

What have you learned?

A Christian congregation can survive and often appear to prosper in the community by the exercise of human talent and without any

touch from the Holy Spirit. But it is simply religious activity, and the dear people will not know anything better until the great and terrible day when our self-employed talents are burned with fire and only what was wrought by the Holy Spirit will stand.
A W Tozer 2

Q Have another look at chapter 1 – *'Who is the Holy Spirit?'* – and share with your group at least one piece of information which was an encouragement to you.

Q Look again at chapter 2 – *'Spiritual gifts – What do I need to know?'* – and write down what has helped you the most in this chapter. (This might be a question/answer, a verse, a quote, or the personal comment.)

Q Look back at chapters 3 to 9. Which of these chapters did you find particularly useful in your understanding of spiritual gifts? Give a reason for your answer.

How will your responses to the above questions influence your life in a practical way? What changes will result as a consequence? *Take time now* to consider the impact of this study on your understanding of spiritual gifts. Give thanks to the Lord that he has given you the gift of himself as well as special gifts to help you to play your part in the life of the church.

How to discover your gift(s)

As we turn from sin and disobedience, and choose to believe in Jesus Christ, trust God in all things, and obey God's commandments and the leading of the Holy Spirit, we are prepared and made 'ready' for service. The Holy Spirit who indwells you as a believer will prepare you for ministry, direct you to ministry, and empower you for ministry.
Charles Stanley 3

In chapter two, we looked briefly at how you might find out what your part in the church is. The following statements might help you even further.

◆ Be willing for God to use you – on his terms. How important do you think this statement is? Give a reason for your answer.

◆ Consciously offer yourself to the Lord. How does Romans 12:1,2 help you to do this?

◆ Review the list of gifts in chapter 2. Which one(s) do you find yourself being particularly drawn to?

◆ Take some time to think about the needs in your church. Which one(s) concern you the most?

Is there any overlap in your answers to the last two questions? For example, you might have put down 'evangelism' as a gift which attracts you, and you might believe that a pressing need in your church is to evangelise the local community. This *might* suggest that you need to explore whether or not evangelism is one of your gifts.

◆ Ask the Lord for wisdom in being able to discover your spiritual gift(s).

Read James 1:5

Q In what way does this encourage you in trying to find out your gift(s)?

Q Look for opportunities to use what might be your possible gift(s). Sometimes the only way to find out whether or not you're spiritually gifted in some area is to try it out! Taking possible gifts you might have already identified, list practical ways in which you could 'try them out'.

Q Carefully evaluate the effects of your ministry. Are others in the church helped by what you do? Do others affirm your giftedness in this particular area? Do you experience fulfilment and satisfaction in what you're doing ie a 'this-is-what-I-was-created-for' response?

Read John 14:21

Q Why is daily obedience in keeping the Lord's commandments important as we go about discovering and developing our spiritual gifts?

The unopened gift

*One of the most sobering aspects of the story is that the servant is judged, not for doing **bad** things, but for doing **nothing**. He didn't steal or embezzle or defraud. He merely buried his gift.*
John Ortberg 4

Picture the scene: you've received a gift from a friend, but you put it – unopened – to one side because you're so busy with your life and just don't have time to open it at the moment. Maybe you intend to unwrap it later on but, somehow, you just never get round to it. Then imagine that at the end of your life, when it is too late, you open this present and find, to your complete amazement, that it contains tools which would have helped you to do various jobs so much more easily and more effectively. With these tools, you could have been more useful to other people, as well as bringing satisfaction to yourself. You – and others – have missed out because you didn't bother to open up your present!

Q Pretend you are the person in the above story and write down what you think might have been your response when you realised, too late, the value of your gift.

Q How do you think the person who gave you the gift would feel if they knew you hadn't taken the time to open the present and thank them for it?

Read Matthew 25:14–30

Q The master gave talents to three of his servants. (Note that talent in this context referred to a weight – the present-day equivalent would probably be different sums of money.) To one he gave five talents, to another he gave two talents, and to the third he gave one talent. Verse 15 says he did this according to the ability of each of the servants. What do you think is the importance of this?

Q How did the first two servants use what they had been given?

Q What did the man who received one talent do with what he had been given?

Q What was the master's response to the first two servants?

Q Does it surprise you that he says exactly the same to both people? Give a reason for your answer.

Read verses 24–30.

Q In what way(s) could this be a picture of an unused spiritual gift? In what way(s) is it probably not?

What are you doing with the gift the Lord has given you? Have you opened it yet? Have you thanked him for it? Are you using it in the way he intended? Is your gift complementing the gifts of others in the church? *Take time now* to answer these questions carefully and prayerfully, asking the Lord to direct you in your service for him. He wants the very best for you – so trust him!

Personal comment

We're strange people, aren't we? We can get ourselves into a way of thinking which suggests that if we enjoy doing something, then it can't possibly be God's will for us. It's as if God is a kill-joy who will only be satisfied if we serve him obediently, but miserably. What a contrast this is to what's expressed in Psalm 40:8 – 'I delight *to do your will, o my God.' One of the exciting things about discovering our spiritual gifts is that using them brings us delight. There's no denying that not everything we do as Christians is like this – there are some things we do out of duty and our hearts aren't really in it – but, in the realm of spiritual gifts, our whole personalities are involved. We need to be passionate about what we're doing and the way we do it. Bruce Bugbee et al define passion as 'the God-given desire that compels us to make a differ-*

ence in a particular ministry'.[5] This desire adds a powerful dimension to our ability to serve God enthusiastically. The way we use our spiritual gifts reflects our personal style. Some individuals are primarily task-oriented; others are mainly people-oriented. In addition, some people like to organise things in a structured way; others in a more unstructured manner. For more on this and spiritual gifts in general, consult Network: The Right People … In the Right Places … For the Right Reasons by Bruce Bugbee et al (see Notes for publication details). Another useful book is Lifekeys: Discovering Who You Are, Why You're Here, What You Do Best by Jane A G Kise et al.[6] Both of these books can be of practical help as you try to discover your spiritual gift(s).

If I were asked to sum up the most important principles from this study, what would I say? Perhaps I'd answer in the following way:

◆ Familiarise yourself with the spiritual gifts which are mentioned in the Bible.

◆ Be open to the Lord as you try to discover which gift(s) he has for you.

◆ Don't demand to have a particular gift – let the Giver decide.

◆ Don't discover your spiritual gift for curiosity's sake – make sure you use your gift with the Lord's help.

◆ Remember that gifts of the Spirit are different from fruit of the Spirit. Read Galatians 5:22,23 to remind yourself of the fruit – in many ways, this is more important than the gifts in that the fruit refers to what a Christian is, ie character, while the gifts refer to what a Christian does, ie usefulness in the church.

◆ Don't ever let spiritual gifts be a reason for bickering and falling out with other Christians – the purpose of gifts is to edify the church, not weaken or destroy it. That's why 1 Corinthians 13 is so important.

I think the phrase 'use it or lose it' is very applicable to spiritual gifts. Let's not neglect this area of biblical teaching – God knows we can't do anything of eternal significance unless he equips us. Our own natural talents, highly developed as they might be, will never compensate for neglecting the specific spiritual gifts which the Lord has given to every Christian believer – have you unwrapped your gift(s) yet?

| Endnotes

Chapter 1

1 Max Anders, *What You Need To Know About The Holy Spirit In 12 Lessons,* Thomas Nelson, 1995, p3.

2 Max Lucado, 'Music for the Dance', *Discipleship Journal,* no. 91 (Jan/Feb 1996).

3 Craig Keener, 'Spirit at Work', *Discipleship Journal,* no. 91 (Jan/Feb 1996).

4 A W Tozer, *How To Be Filled With The Holy Spirit,* Christian Publications, pp38,39.

5 Billy Graham, *The Holy Spirit,* Marshall Pickering, 1995, p118.

6 Billy Graham, *The Holy Spirit,* Marshall Pickering, 1995, p125.

Chapter 2

1 A W Tozer, *Leaning Into The Wind,* Kingsway, 1985, p47.

2 Bruce Bugbee, Don Cousins, and Bill Hybels, *Network: Participant's Guide,* Zondervan Publishing House, 1994, p32.

3 Susan Maycinik, 'How Many Gifts Are There?' *Discipleship Journal,* no. 90 (Nov/Dec 1995).

4 Bruce Bugbee, Don Cousins, and Bill Hybels, *Network: Participant's Guide,* Zondervan Publishing House, 1994, pp30–32.

5 Warren W Wiersbe, *With The Word,* Thomas Nelson, 1991, p752.

6 Jim Burns and Doug Fields, *The Word On Finding And Using Your Spiritual Gifts,* Youthbuilders Group Bible Studies, Gospel Light, 1995, p39.

7 J I Packer, 'The Empowered Christian Life' in Gary S Greig and Kevin N Springer, *The Kingdom and the Power,* Gospel Light/Regal Books, 1993. Used with permission.

Chapter 3

1 Kenneth C Kinghorn, *Gifts of the Spirit,* Abingdon, 1976, p30.

2 *Life Application Study Bible: New Living Translation,* Tyndale House, 1996, p1699.

3 Jane A G Kise, David Stark and Sandra Krebs Hirsh, *Lifekeys: Discovering Who You Are, Why You're Here, What You Do Best,* Bethany House, 1996, p71.

4 *Life Application Study Bible: New Living Translation,* Tyndale House, 1996, p359.

5 Jane A G Kise, David Stark and Sandra Krebs Hirsh, *Lifekeys: Discovering Who You

Are, Why You're Here, What You Do Best, Bethany House, 1996, p99.

6 Lynne and Bill Hybels, *Rediscovering Church,* Zondervan, 1995, p152.

7 Bruce Bugbee, Don Cousins and Bill Hybels, *Network: The Right People … In the Right Place s… For the Right Reasons,* Zondervan, 1994, p76.

8 Jane A G Kise, David Stark and Sandra Krebs Hirsh, *Lifekeys: Discovering Who You Are, Why You're Here, What You Do Best,* Bethany House, 1996, p73.

9 Kenneth C Kinghorn, *Gifts of the Spirit,* Abingdon, 1976, p47.

Chapter 4

1 A W Tozer, *Tragedy in the Church: The Missing Gifts,* Christian Publications, 1990, pp25,26.

2 'The Year's Best Headlines' The remarkable site. www.marklowry.com/funnies/headlines.html

3 *Life Application Study Bible: New Living Translation,* Tyndale House, 1996, p1707.

4 Leslie Flynn, *19 Gifts of the Spirit,* Communication Ministries, 1996. Used with permission. All Rights Reserved.

5 Kenneth C Kinghorn, *Gifts of the Spirit,* Abingdon, 1976, p51.

6 Billy Graham, *The Holy Spirit,* Marshall Pickering, 1995, p146.

7 Bruce Bugbee, Don Cousins and Bill Hybels, *Network: The Right People … In the Right Places … For the Right Reasons,* Zondervan Publishing House, 1994, p93.

8 Gilbert Bilezikian, *Beyond Sex Roles,* Baker Book House, 1985, pp201,202.

9 Bruce Bugbee, Don Cousins and Bill Hybels, *Network: The Right People … In the Right Places … For the Right Reasons,* Zondervan Publishing House, 1994, p95.

10 Jim Covell, Karen Covell and Victorya Michaels Rogers, *How To Talk About Jesus Without Freaking Out,* Multnomah, 2000.

Chapter 5

1 Jill Briscoe, 'Deborah – How To Fight Your Battles' from the audiocassette series *Women Who Changed Their World,* Telling the Truth.

2 C Peter Wagner, *Your Spiritual Gifts Can Help Your Church Grow,* Gospel Light/Regal Books, 1994, p192,193. Used with permission.

3 Kenneth Kinghorn, *Gifts of the Spirit,* Abingdon, 1976, p61.

4 *Life Application Study Bible: New Living Translation,* Tyndale House, 1996, p1697.

5 Jim Burns and Doug Fields, *The Word On Finding And Using Your Spiritual Gifts,* Youthbuilders Group Bible Studies, Gospel Light, 1995, p39. Copyright AMG International. All rights reserved. Used with permission.

6 Profiles: Unwrapping Your Spiritual Gifts, *Discipleship Journal,* no. 90 (Nov/Dec 1995).

7 Kenneth C Kinghorn, *Gifts of the Spirit,* Abingdon, 1976, p82.

8 Phyllis Bennett, *Discovering Your Spiritual Gifts,* Women of Faith Bible Study Series, Zondervan, 1998, p30.

Chapter 6

1   Kenneth C Kinghorn, *Gifts of the Spirit*, Abingdon, 1976, p94.

2   Lois Mowday Rabey, 'The Power of Encouragement', *Discipleship Journal* no. 97 (Jan/Feb 1997).

3   Phyllis Bennett, *Discovering Your Spiritual Gifts*, Women of Faith Bible Study Series, Zondervan, 1998, p29.

4   C Peter Wagner, *Your Spiritual Gifts Can Help Your Church Grow*, Gospel Light/Regal Books, 1994, p194. Used with permission.

5   C Peter Wagner *Your Spiritual Gifts Can Help Your Church Grow*, Gospel Light/Regal Books, 1994, p195. Used with permission.

6   Billy Graham, *The Holy Spirit*, Marshall Pickering, 1995, p152.

7   Jane A G Kise, David Stark and Sandra Krebs Hirsh, *Lifekeys: Discovering Who You Are, Why You're Here, What You Do Best*, Bethany House Publishers, 1996, p108.

Chapter 7

1   Steven C Lombardo, 'Beware The Limelight', *Discipleship Journal*, no. 23 (Sept/Oct 1984).

2   Gracie Malone, 'Can You Spare Some Change?' *Discipleship Journal*, no. 106 (Jul/Aug 1998).

3   Bruce Bugbee, Don Cousins, Bill Hybels, *Network: The Right People ... In the Right Places ... For the Right Reasons*, Zondervan, 1994, p83.

4   Jim Burns and Doug Fields, *The Word On Finding And Using Your Spiritual Gifts*, Youthbuilders Group Bible Studies, Gospel Light/Regal Books, 1995, p115. Used with permission.

5   Jane A G Kise, David Start and Sandra Krebs Hirsh, *Lifekeys: Discovering Who You Are, Why You're Here, What You Do Best*, Bethany House, 1996, p92.

6   Ray Hoo, 'Turn Your World Upside Down', *Discipleship Journal*, no. 10 (July/Aug 1982).

7   C Peter Wagner, *Your Spiritual Gifts Can Help Your Church Grow*, Gospel Light/Regal Books, 1994, pp197,198. Used with permission.

Chapter 8

1   Brad Atkins, 'Why Aren't We Moving Mountains?' *Discipleship Journal*, issue no. 10 (July/Aug 1982).

2   Martha E Chamberlain, 'Asking For A Miracle', *Discipleship Journal*, no. 41 (Sep/Oct 1987).

3   Leslie Flynn, *19 Gifts of the Spirit*, Communications Ministries, 1996, p157. Used with permission. All rights reserved.

4   Leslie Flynn *19 Gifts of the Spirit*, Communications Ministries, 1996, p192. Used with permission. All rights reserved.

5 Bruce Bugbee, Don Cousins and Bill Hybels, *Network: The Right People ... In The Right Places ... For The Right Reasons,* Zondervan Publishing House, 1994, p84.

6 Jane A G Kise, David Stark and Sandra Krebs Hirsh, *Lifekeys: Discovering Who You Are, Why You're Here, What You Do Best,* Bethany House Publishers, 1996, p90.

7 Billy Graham, *The Holy Spirit,* Marshall Pickering, 1995, p174,5.

8 Phyllis Bennett, *Discovering Your Spiritual Gifts,* Women of Faith Bible Study Series, Zondervan, 1998, p42.

Chapter 9

1 Kenneth C Kinghorn, *Gifts of the Spirit,* Abingdon, 1976, pp103,104.

2 Billy Graham, *The Holy Spirit,* Marshall Pickering, 1978, p188.

3 Phyllis Bennett, *Discovering Your Spiritual Gifts,* Women of Faith Bible Study Series, Zondervan, 1998, p31.

4 Kenneth C Kinghorn, *Gifts of the Spirit,* Abingdon, 1976, p104.

5 Ralph Ennis, *Breakthru: A Spiritual Gifts Diagnostic Inventory,* LEAD Consulting, 1991, p16. Used with permission.

6 Billy Graham, *The Holy Spirit,* Marshall Pickering, 1995, p187.

Chapter 10

1 John Ortberg, *If You Want To Walk On Water You've Got To Get Out Of The Boat,* Zondervan, 2001, p43.

2 A W Tozer, *Tragedy In The Church,* Christian Publications, 1990, p23.

3 Charles Stanley, *Ministering Through Spiritual Gifts,* Thomas Nelson, 1999, p105.

4 John Ortberg, *If You Want To Walk On Water You've Got To Get Out Of The Boat,* Zondervan, 2001, p45.

5 Bruce Bugbee, Don Cousins and Bill Hybels, *Network: The Right People ... In The Right Places ... For The Right Reasons,* Zondervan, 1994.

6 Jane A G Kise, David Stark and Sandra Krebs Hirsh, *Lifekeys: Discovering Who You Are, Why You're Here, What You Do Best,* Bethany House, 1996.